NAIS

Journal of the NATIVE AMERICAN *and*
INDIGENOUS STUDIES ASSOCIATION

VOLUME 4.2

2017

NAIS (ISSN 2332-1261) is published two times a year by the University of Minnesota Press, 111 Third Avenue South, Suite 290, Minneapolis, MN 55401-2520. http://www.upress.umn.edu

Postmaster: Send address changes to *NAIS,* University of Minnesota Press, 111 Third Avenue South, Suite 290, Minneapolis, MN 55401-2520.

Information about manuscript submissions can be found at naisa.org, or inquiries can be sent to journal@naisa.org.

Books and other material for review should be addressed to *NAIS*, Department of American Studies, University of Kansas, Bailey Hall, Room 213, 1440 Jayhawk Boulevard, Lawrence, KS 66045-7594.

Address subscription orders, changes of address, and business correspondence (including requests for permission and advertising orders) to *NAIS,* University of Minnesota Press, 111 Third Avenue South, Suite 290, Minneapolis, MN 55401-2520.

SUBSCRIPTIONS

- **Individual subscriptions to *NAIS*** are a benefit of membership in the Native American and Indigenous Studies Association. NAISA membership is $50 annually. To become a member, visit http://naisa.org/.
- **Institutional subscriptions to *NAIS*** are $100 inside the U.S., $105 outside the U.S. Checks should be made payable to the University of Minnesota Press and sent to *NAIS,* University of Minnesota Press, 111 Third Avenue South, Suite 290, Minneapolis, MN 55401-2520.
- **Back issues of *NAIS*** are $25 for individuals (plus $6.00 shipping for the first copy, $1.25 for each additional copy inside the U.S.A.; $9.50 shipping for the first copy, $6 for each additional copy, outside the U.S.A.).
- **Digital subscriptions to *NAIS* for institutions** are available online through the JSTOR Current Scholarship Program at http://www.jstor.org/r/umnpress.

NAIS

Journal of the NATIVE AMERICAN *and* INDIGENOUS STUDIES ASSOCIATION

CONTENTS
VOLUME 4 ● ISSUE 2

2017

IOKEPA CASUMBAL-SALAZAR

A Fictive Kinship: Making "Modernity," "Ancient Hawaiians," and the Telescopes on Mauna Kea

The University of Hawaii continues to believe that Mauna Kea is a precious resource where science and culture can synergistically coexist, now and into the future, and remains strongly in support of the Thirty Meter Telescope.
 —DAN MEISENZAHL, QUOTED IN THE *HONOLULU CIVIL BEAT*

Unfortunately there's this whole colonialism thing going on, and so, you have to, somehow, get past that. It's kind of easy for us [astronomers] to get past that because I don't feel like a colonial person. . . . I feel like I'm one of the slaves. . . . From the astronomy perspective it's less of a big leap to get over that.
 —PAUL COLEMAN, INTERVIEW BY AUTHOR, MAY 8, 2013

It has nothing to do with astronomy. You could build anything up there. The problem is that you want to build anything up there.
 —ABRAHAM KAMAKAWIWOʻOLE, QUOTED IN *MAUNA KEA: TEMPLE UNDER SIEGE*

WHAT CAN MAUNA KEA TEACH US about settler colonialism in Hawaiʻi? This article analyzes the politics and poetics of the struggle over Mauna a Wākea and the Thirty Meter Telescope (or TMT)—a $1.4 billion observatory boasting to be the next "world's largest telescope," proposed for construction on the mountain considered sacred to Kanaka ʻŌiwi (Native Hawaiians), that, if built, would become the summit's fourteenth.[1] It would stand eighteen stories tall, displace roughly ten acres of undisturbed land on the mountain's northern plateau, and dig one hundred feet below the earth's surface, possibly more. While many Kanaka ʻŌiwi argue the TMT would desecrate one of the most sacred sites in the islands—a place revered as a house of worship, an ancestor, and an elder sibling in the moʻokūʻauhau (or genealogical succession) of all Hawaiians—advocates of big science justify the transgression by lauding the project's pledge to create jobs, stimulate the economy, and fund educational opportunities in STEM. Others repeat the promise of new discoveries that will explain the origins of our universe: a scientific ambition thought to generate myriad benefits for all of humanity. Yet, as TMT advocates emphasize the project's urgency, they also insist that the Western imperative of "modern astronomy" to explore space is analogous to "ancient Hawaiian" sea voyaging in the Pacific. The discursive strategy consigns indigeneity to obsolescence. While Western science is conflated with modernity and settler culture is imagined as the measure of humanity, Kānaka 'Ōiwi who oppose the TMT are rendered selfish, regressive, and unreasonable. Likewise, TMT proponents argue that exploration of new frontiers and discovery of distant worlds is a universal human aspiration. I argue that the ideologies of science and multiculturalism in which these assumptions are embedded function to delimit what constitutes rationality and, thus, the category of the human. I explain how, within the hierarchies of human difference these discourses conjure, Kanaka 'Ōiwi appear as a foil to the scientific settler state's legitimacy as sovereign and desire to become native. I will also show how the struggle to protect Mauna a Wākea is emblematic of over a century of struggle against U.S. settler colonialism, its logic of elimination, and practices of replacement.[2]

In examining this controversy, I might have challenged the allocation of public and private resources channeled into big science projects while poverty persists, health care and education remain inaccessible to many, and the state's dependency on tourism and militarism has produced enormous wealth disparities, widespread homelessness, and Kanaka emigration. Instead, however, my focus here is directed toward ideologies of discovery, belonging, possession, and knowledge. I am concerned with ways in which the rhetoric of big science, as taken up by the state and advocates of astronomy expansion, works to expel Kanaka 'Ōiwi from modernity as a path to settler selfhood. Within the official narrative practices that dimly repeat the ambiguous categories and cultural imperatives to "discover new worlds," advance "scientific knowledge," and "coexist on the mountain," particularly when combined with the state's legal apparatus, Kanaka 'Ōiwi are ruled ineligible as caretakers of land and, thus, are denied a meaningful voice in decisions over the future of Hawai'i. Relegated to the "dark ages" of tradition, Native peoples appear as the agonistic menace of the modern scientific state. Delegitimized as irrational within the gendered hierarchies of Western science and philosophy— both of which bear heavily on contemporary views of Indigenous culture and activism—Hawaiians become suspect and subject to institutional anti-Native racism yet fetishized as an archeological remnant within multicultural society. Looking at narrative practices by which 'Ōiwi are disqualified and settler legitimacy is achieved, I argue that the urgency for another telescope is less about progress or the human condition than maintaining control over land and confining Native self-determination to a permanent state of deferral. With Mauna Kea, the co-constitution of Western sciences and imperialism is laid bare. Though, as ʻŌiwi philosopher Manulani Meyer describes it, Mauna a Wākea "is a perfect example of clashing cosmologies,"[3] it is also an example of the mechanics of settler colonialism. Before I discuss the historical context of the current struggle, let me begin with a scene of Kanaka ʻŌiwi resurgence.

Kū Kiaʻi Mauna

Outraged by the Board of Land and Natural Resources' final decision to uphold a permit issued to the University of Hawaiʻi for construction of the Thirty Meter Telescope in 2013, Kānaka ʻŌiwi took to the mountain in October 2014 and again in April 2015. With the permit awarded, many thought construction of the TMT was inevitable, until a group of Kanaka ʻŌiwi activists in their twenties—educated and fluent in our language, culture, and history—decided to put their bodies on the line in defense of the sacred mauna. What began as a small but dogged effort to block the delivery of heavy equipment from reaching the summit quickly exploded into a six-month mass demonstration on the mountain. Within days, the TMT controversy was thrust into the global media spotlight. It was almost impossible to miss reports of the daily confrontations between state park rangers, county police, Office of Mauna Kea Management personnel, and land defenders.

Initially, spontaneous roadblocks and vehicle checkpoints were fashioned to keep work crews from reaching the project site, but very shortly a semipermanent encampment went up. In Hawaiian a kiaʻi is a guardian or caretaker. As the media began covering the activists' actions as "protests," it became clear the underlying connotation was that "protestors" were unreasonable, ill-informed, and petulant. This image was reinforced in the contested case hearings as well, as the University of Hawaiʻi had actual legal teams while those petitioning the permit were ordinary, untrained citizens. Immediately they began self-identifying as kiaʻi, or protectors, instead of conceding to the diminutive referent and thereby reshaping the public debate. The kiaʻi were not fighting against something so much as they were fighting *for something*: the protection of the mountain from further development. The demonstration culminated on June 24 with a dramatic, daylong standoff in which dozens of kiaʻi were arrested. Over seven hundred people participated in the action that day. A series of arms-linked human blockades were positioned across the road to the summit, each functioning as a distinct front that would slow the police caravan, stall arrests, and undermine any notion that removal would be swift and simple. The first to confront police was a line of ʻŌiwi women, who invoked the female kupua (demigod, supernatural being) of Mauna Kea and chanted their resolve. Eventually, once the first few lines of kiaʻi had been overcome, they scattered large stones across the unpaved road, disabling the officers' vehicles from advancing. As the mist of Lilinoe shrouded the summit, construction crews and law enforcement descended the mountain in defeat.

Throughout the summer there were several more confrontations. A set of "emergency rules" that included a ban on overnight camping was ordered by governor David Ige as an attempt to dismantle the activists' encampment. This led to one nighttime raid in which seven women in prayer and ceremony were arrested without warning. Yet, simultaneously throughout local communities, solidarity actions across every island began breaking out as well. There was also an unprecedented proliferation of news coverage across the United States and abroad as well as an increase in scholarly attention unseen over the previous decade of Mauna Kea activism. The hashtags #WeAreMaunaKea, #KūKiaʻiMauna (rise protectors of the mountain), #AoleTMT (No TMT), and #ProtectMaunaKea went viral over social media, attracting celebrities and other supporters from around the world.

By December the spectacle of an Indigenous uprising incited the Hawaiʻi State Supreme Court to review and revoke the TMT's permit (discussed below). However, the victory was bittersweet, as the decision to rescind the permit was justified, *not* because of the project's ethical, cultural, or environmental transgressions, but instead because the permit was granted *prior* to holding a contested case hearing. In a procedural error, the state's Board of Land and Natural Resources had simply failed to observe due process. This was a precarious victory, as the court's ruling was less a turn toward justice than a political act. Though aligned with the demands of Kanaka ʻŌiwi and our allies, it was ultimately a re-inscription of state authority. While most TMT opponents welcome the decision, I fear the state has nevertheless retained something far more valuable than a telescope: its authority to decide.[4] Next, I explain how the mountain is sacred within Kanaka ontologies to provide context for why Hawaiians have chosen to use their bodies, where their voices were ignored, in defense of this place.

ʻO ke keiki pō lani kēia a Kea i hānau: The Sacred Mauna

Mauna Kea is commonly translated as the "white mountain" because of its snowcapped peaks during winter months and the word "kea" translates as "white," but its name has other meanings as well.[5] It is also the namesake of the akua (god), Wākea (the expanse of the sky), hence today's popular name, Mauna a Wākea. The mountain is also the hiapo (firstborn) of the five mountain peaks born to Papahānaumoku (Papa who gives birth to islands). Also referred to as "Earth Mother" and "Sky Father," Papa and Wākea are two of three original ancestors in the epic moʻokūʻauhau (genealogical succession) known as the Kumulipo, which ties Kanaka ʻŌiwi to ʻāina, the land, in a familial relationship. Preceding written literature, the Kumulipo is a koʻihonua, or cosmogonical mele (chant), that is structured around scientific observation of environmental and celestial patterns. It describes the origins of the universe[6] beginning in the time and space of Pō (darkness) and mapping the emergence of all elemental forms—animate and inanimate—from the smallest of creatures to the stars, to humans, and beyond. In this moʻokūʻauhau, Papa, Wākea, and their daughter, Hoʻohōkūkalani ("she who creates stars in the sky"), are parents of the archipelago, the makaʻāinana (the common people), and the aliʻi (the ruling class).[7] Hoʻohōkūkalani births Hāloanakalaukapalili (quivering long stalk), a premature son born still and from whose burial place emerged the first kalo (taro), the staple food of Kanaka that allowed for the Lāhui (the nation and people) to flourish. The second son, Hāloa, named after his elder sibling, was the first human and the first aliʻi to govern the Lāhui. These connections were attached to the genealogy of aliʻi to emphasize the centrality of environmental responsibility and resource management to the idea of good governance. As Noenoe Silva argues, these moʻolelo (stories, histories) "are ingeniously crafted metaphors. They are carrying substantial symbolic weight and are also indicative of a way of being in the world and of conceiving the world and our place in it—we are part of a family that includes the sun, stars, ocean, and everything else in the world." The moʻokūʻauhau also conveys the kuleana (right, privilege, responsibility) Kanaka ʻŌiwi are encouraged to adopt and practice—that is, to care for the land as a member of one's family. While Mauna Kea is conceived as an elder sibling, an ancestor, in a genealogy that includes the aliʻi, the makaʻāinana, and ʻāina, many today use the name "Mauna a Wākea," or "the mountain belonging to Wākea."[8]

Mauna a Wākea is also a piko. Translated as both "summit" and "umbilicus," piko describes the mountain and connotes its generative life forces. The human body has three piko: the crown of the head, the navel/umbilical cord, and the genitals. The concept of a piko also signifies genealogical connection, referring to a spiritual center, a "linking of the body with forebears of old and descendants to come."[9] For many of the families living on the slopes of Mauna a Wākea, a very old tradition that continues today is the practice of depositing the piko and ʻiewe (afterbirth, placenta) of the family's newborn in hidden places on the summit to protect the child. For this reason, the mauna was also known as "ka piko kaulana o ka ʻāina," the *famous piko of the land*."[10]

As the fresh water of Mauna a Wākea produces rich soil for much of Hawaiʻi Island, ʻŌiwi also honor its significance as a source of life by celebrating its many water forms—the mist, rains, clouds, the lake, and the snow. It is no coincidence that the spirits attached to these water forms are frequently women—the akua and kupua said to live on Mauna a Wākea, including Lilinoe,

Waiau,[11] Poliʻahu, Kahoupokane, and Moʻoinanea. Although its namesake is Wākea, the mountain is also famous for the mana wahine (female power) it celebrates through such naming practices. For the descendants of Papa, Hoʻohōkūkalani, and Wākea, Mauna a Wākea is "the ʻaha hoʻowili moʻo (the genealogical cord) that ties earth to the heavens,"[12] symbolizing "the bonds between the living individual and . . . [one's] never known and long departed ancestors."[13] It is, at once, an ancestor, a portal to the akua, an elder sibling, a primary source of water for the people, and a place of spiritual being and reflection for Kanaka ʻŌiwi. This body of thought and way of relating to the natural world is part of a deeply held ethical positionality common to many ʻŌiwi, what I describe as an onto-genealogical ethos: that is, to care for the land, water, and other natural beings. In many ways, it is this conception of being and ethic of cherishing the land that constitutes the foundation of what we call aloha ʻāina—a key concept in ʻŌiwi thought (to which I will return).

Mauna a Wākea is located in a region of the mauna (mountain) called kuahea, or an "area where trees are stunted as due to altitude," far above elevations habitable for human populations.[14] In kuahea, thin air deprives the lungs of oxygen, sunlight is harsh to the skin, the cold is piercing, and few plant or animal siblings can live.[15] Measured from ocean floor to its peak at 33,474 feet, Mauna a Wākea is the tallest mountain on the planet. At this elevation, altitude sickness is common: CO_2 drops and gas molecules expand, causing stomach cramps, lightheadedness, dehydration, fainting, headaches, vomiting, nausea, or worse. For those who make the journey, there are major health risks involved. For ʻŌiwi i ka wā kahiko (in the times of old), these effects on the body must have contributed to its mana (divine power) and the sense of reverence, humility, and respect with which ʻŌiwi related to the mountain. The layers upon layers of meaning attributed to this place represent an ʻŌiwi ontological relationship to Mauna a Wākea and a way of being in the world that renders the land as family. This is why Mauna a Wākea is sacred.

Half a Century of Astronomy and Mismanagement on Mauna a Wākea

Astronomers say that to understand the origins and evolution of the universe, they must study the oldest, most distant light. To probe further into space, there is a constant demand for bigger, faster, and more powerful telescopes. Many of the world's best observatories are currently located on Mauna Kea. Over the last thirty years great advances in technology have resulted in major scientific breakthroughs among the telescopes. For example, observations made at the Keck Observatory[16] have led to the discovery of dwarf planets, the approximate age of the observable universe, and the rate at which the universe is expanding. Yet, more answers lead to more questions. With technology advancing as quickly as it does and with the most cutting-edge telescopes reaching their limits, many scientists suggest that the only solution is to build more powerful instruments, like the Thirty Meter Telescope. The TMT promises to render distant objects that were previously inaccessible, not only visible, but with greater speed and clarity. With millions of dollars already committed to the project, over a decade of planning, and parts being manufactured around the world, as of this writing all that remains is the state of Hawaiʻi conservation district use permit.

In 1968 the University of Hawaiʻi entered into a sixty-five-year lease with the state, paying a nominal one dollar per year to use 13,321 acres of summit lands situated in the ahupuaʻa (division) of Kaʻohe in the mokuoloko (district) of Hāmākua to build a "an observatory."[17] The first telescope was erected that year; and every decade since, UH has continued to grow its astronomy franchise. Four successive telescopes were built in the 1970s and, at that time, there was no public consultation, no clear management process, and little governmental oversight.[18] In the 1980s, two more telescopes went up and a third broke ground, while no binding management plan was approved by the state Department of Land and Natural Resources until 1985; moreover, even this UH Mauna Kea Management Plan and its 1995 Revised Management Plan failed to address the adverse impacts of continued industrial development on the ecological or historical properties of the summit or the lives, cultural practices, and well-being of Kanaka ʻŌiwi. In 1961, HRS 183 was passed into law through Act 187, which created the four major land districts—Conservation, Agricultural, Rural, and Urban—encompassing all land in the state. However, it was not until HRS 183c, passed by Act 270 in 1994, that the state would retroactively make the telescopes legal vis-à-vis its newly created "resource subzone"—one of five categories within the Conservation District—for which the category "astronomy facilities" was conjured as an approved land use. This means that the laws making astronomy on Mauna Kea legal were written after the Conservation District laws—after seven telescopes were already built. The Final EIS suggests there are currently "12 facilities" on the summit, "11 observatories and one separate telescope."[19] Because the Keck Observatory and the Submillimeter Array, which consists of eight mobile dishes, are each considered by the University of Hawaiʻi to be a single "observatory," what amounts to twenty-one telescopes has been reduced to a count of thirteen.

Mauna Kea is prized by astronomers because of its unparalleled physical attributes. It is the tallest mountain on earth as measured from the ocean floor to its peak. At 13,796 feet in elevation and surrounded by thousands of miles of open ocean, there is very little atmospheric turbulence. Rising to over 40 percent of the earth's atmosphere, the air is extremely stable, dry, and cold—essential qualities for ground-based observation. Piercing above the general cloud layer, the mountain has a relatively high number of clear nights annually. Compared to other more remote locations such as those in Chile or South Africa, Mauna Kea is also rather accessible, being less than two hours from Hilo and five hours from the mainland United States.

One scientist told me that astronomy is a "benign science" because it is based on observation, and that it is universally beneficial because it offers "basic human knowledge" that everyone should know "like human anatomy." Such a statement underscores the cultural bias within conventional notions of what constitutes the "human" and "knowledge." In the absence of a critical self-reflection on this inherent ethnocentrism, the tacit claim to universal truth reproduces the cultural supremacy of Western science as self-evident. Here, the needs of astronomers for tall peaks in remote locations supplant the needs of Indigenous communities on whose ancestral territories these observatories are built. It does so by invoking the morality of liberal multiculturalism. "Why would anyone oppose astronomy? Why are Hawaiians standing in the way of progress?" they ask. "Can't astronomers and Hawaiians coexist on the mountain?" These frames decontextualize the historical relations in which the TMT controversy has emerged and dehistoricize the struggle over land and resources in Hawai'i by vacating discourse on settler colonialism in favor of problematic claims to universality. When the opposition to the TMT is misrepresented as an arbitrary disregard for science, Hawaiians appear unreasonably obstinate. In light of the stories of U.S. imperialism in Oceania and Hawai'i, perhaps we should be asking, *What* constitutes progress? *Who* determines that? And *what* are the costs of its production?

In 1959, as a condition of statehood, the territorial government was to assume a relationship of guardianship over Native Hawaiians, an arrangement in which Indigenous calls for independent governance was ignored.[20] According to this protectorate relationship, Native Hawaiians are like wards of a court—they cannot sue the U.S. government for misuse of lands or violation of rights. Hawaiians have no land base but retain a one-fifth interest in the "Ceded Lands."[21] They receive a portion of revenues generated from what totals approximately 1.8 million acres of former Hawaiian Kingdom government and Crown lands that were seized in 1893 by a group of conspirators who would soon fashion themselves the "Republic of Hawaii." To avoid prosecution for treason should the legitimate government return to power, the conspirators "transferred" these lands—the spoils of a foreign intervention—to the United States under the auspices of "annexation" in 1898.[22] The lands were then renamed "Public Lands," to be controlled by the government of the Territory of Hawaiʻi. When Hawaiʻi was made a state in 1959, authority over these lands was then transferred to the state of Hawaiʻi, which has held them as a "public trust" for five purposes, one of those being the betterment of Native Hawaiians.[23] Aside from the hegemony secured through U.S. military occupation, the state's authority comes mainly from the perception of its legitimacy, which derives from its mandate to manage Native Hawaiians and the seized lands. Yet, with each new category applied to the Crown and government lands of the Hawaiian Kingdom, the original desception grows more egregious when the legal history the United States' occupation becomes visible.

The first two decades of Hawaiʻi's statehood was a time in which Kanaka ʻŌiwi were fighting dozens of other battles aside from Mauna Kea astronomy. These included struggles over Native rights, access to land and resources, legal protections for cultural practices, and the right to teach ʻŌiwi children in the Hawaiian language. Contrary to popular (and self-affirming) settler claims, Kanaka ʻŌiwi in the 1960s and 1970s did not simply ignore the desecration of Mauna Kea or consent to the development of the mountain. Indeed, Hawaiians expressed their dissent in the few public forums available, by writing newspaper editorials, publishing opinion pieces, and speaking out at public events. However, this generation of Hawaiians was also just beginning to develop a sense of community activism and to heal from the despair and self-doubt caused by nearly a century of U.S. colonial occupation and racist settler hegemony.[24] What came to be known as the Hawaiian Renaissance— a movement inspired by the American civil rights struggles and the antiwar, black, women's, gay, American Indian, and other social movements of the 1960s—would usher in a new era of Native cultural revitalization in arts, sciences, language, dance, history, and other traditional knowledge as well as a collective pride and self-confidence among younger Kanaka.[25] This increasing knowledge of self has resulted in a broad understanding of the systemic injustices under settler colonialism. Since mid-century, the sustained commitment to anticolonial resistance and Indigenous resurgence has only intensified.

Kanaka ʻŌiwi researcher and professor of Indigenous politics Noenoe Silva's discovery of the Kūʻē petitions (also known as the "anti-annexation petitions") in U.S. Library of Congress archives in the early 1990s—by which the signatures of thirty-eight thousand Kingdom citizens blocked ratification of two treaty attempts to annex Hawaiʻi and forced Congress to violate U.S. constitutional and international laws—gave new meaning to Hawaiian activism. If earlier generations had any doubt their sense of injustice and desire for independence were justified, throughout the 1990s and 2000s Kanaka ʻŌiwi would gain strength from this new historical understanding. It told young Kanaka that if their ancestors could fight and succeed in defeating legal annexation of their country, so could they. Organized opposition to astronomy expansion would build momentum in this climate of increasing Indigenous political consciousness.

While the first five telescopes were erected with only limited media attention and legal scrutiny, Kanaka were fighting desecrations, settlements, removals, and other battles around the islands. Among them was the struggle to end the U.S. Navy's bombing of the island of Kahoʻolawe, which it used as target practice for over forty years. While the state of Hawaiʻi leased the mountain's summit lands to the University for a dollar per year, ʻŌiwi fought the rampant tourism development and the mass evictions that drove thousands from Hawaiʻi's beaches, urban centers, and valleys to locations less desired by settlers, developers, and the state.

Through the 1990s, as the encroachments and dispossessions become increasingly glaring and intolerable, a collective desire for justice and political transformation grew into the "Hawaiian sovereignty movement." This history is beyond the scope of the present article, but suffice it to say Kanaka ʻŌiwi had developed a political consciousness that honored the nineteenth-century kupuna who participated in the Kūʻē petition drives. The momentum of a 1993 centennial observance of the U.S. invasion that unseated Queen Liliʻuokalani would build into what Haunani-Kay Trask describes as "the contemporary Hawaiian movement"—a vibrant and decentralized campaign for justice, land, and restoration of independence that persists to this day.[26]

It is in this context the University of Hawaiʻi found itself struggling to gain popular support for its astronomy franchise that had not been required during the first twenty years of construction on the mountain. While Kanaka ʻŌiwi were building an activist consciousness and politics of resistance, they were also becoming lawyers, educators, and defenders of sacred lands, eventually turning their attention toward Mauna Kea. In 1998, a damaging state legislative audit found that after thirty years of construction on the mountain, the University of Hawaiʻi's management was "inadequate to ensure the protection of natural resources," controls were "late and weakly implemented," historical preservation was "neglected," and the "cultural value of Mauna Kea was largely unrecognized."[27] A lengthy federal lawsuit against NASA followed and, in 2003, the Keck Outrigger Telescopes project was defeated when U.S. District Court judge Susan Mollway rejected NASA's environmental assessment for the project because of its failure to adequately address the cumulative impacts of astronomy on Mauna Kea. In 2003, following a contested case hearing, the state's Board of Land and Natural Resources (BLNR) issued a conservation district use permit that allowed astronomy development to continue without a comprehensive management plan. In 2004, community groups appealed to the Third Circuit Court and, in 2005, state lawmakers ordered a follow-up legislative audit, which found that three decades of astronomy activity had caused "significant, substantial and adverse" harm to the "resources" of the summit. In 2006, state Court of Appeal judge Glenn Hara ruled that no further astronomy development on Mauna Kea may be conducted without approval of a comprehensive management plan by the Department of Land and Natural Resources. NASA then withdrew funding for the Keck Outrigger project and the University of Hawai'i began work on developing the most comprehensive management plan (CMP) for Mauna Kea to date. The CMP and its four subplans (the public access plan, the natural resources management plan, the cultural resources management plan, and the decommissioning plan) were thought to cross every "t" and dot every "i" such that it should be almost impossible *not* to permit the TMT. The thousand-plus-page document proscribes no limits on future astronomy development.

To this point, nothing had much interfered with astronomy on the mountain. But now the astronomy community and UH were forced to present themselves as having evolved. They began using the term "cultural sensitivity" in describing how they had turned over a new leaf, reflected on their mistakes, and were now committed to doing the TMT "the right way." They embarked on a lengthy and expensive campaign to assuage community concerns about impacts to the environment by committing to "mitigation measures," actions claiming to offset the anticipated damage to the mountain's natural, cultural, and historical resources. These measures include establishing a "community benefits package" of $1 million a year to be spent on science education in Hawai'i schools. They promise to cover the observatory dome with an "aluminum-like coating," which is supposed to camouflage the structure by reflecting the blue sky. Works by Native Hawaiian artists will hang from interior walls, and select Kānaka 'Ōiwi have been consulted, with some even sitting on the Kahu Kū Mauna advisory board.

Moreover, with the Thirty Meter Telescope under serious consideration and their reputation tanking, advocates of astronomy expansion had to disqualify Hawaiians legally while demonstrating they were giving adequate attention to Hawaiian concerns. They adopted a multicultural model of inclusion, locating Hawaiians who believe "a seat at the table" is better than having no say at all. The CMP used Hawaiian language, histories, and culture to help convince the BLNR and the public that the University of Hawai'i's administration and Institute for Astronomy and the TMT Corporation were committed to the strongest stewardship of the mountain ever known. The management plan was meant to demonstrate a newfound sense of cultural awareness, accountability, transparency, and sensitivity toward Native Hawaiians. The rhetoric of inclusion, participation, and recognition characteristic of liberal multiculturalism would become instrumental in casting skepticism on Kanaka 'Ōiwi activism and the community's calls for protection of the mountain.

In 2009, amid growing protests, the BLNR approved the University of Hawai'i's CMP but denied community requests for a contested case hearing. In 2010, the University of Hawai'i at Hilo applied for a conservation district use permit (CDUP) to build the TMT. The BLNR approved a permit in February 2011, prior to holding a contested case hearing, which was deferred until August. Despite the tenacity of the citizens participating in the contested case— underdogs with no legal expertise facing off against the University's experienced team of professional lawyers—the BLNR's final decision to uphold the permit was delivered in April 2013. At the close of the contested case, hearings officer Paul Aoki justified his ruling by suggesting, "The purpose of the conservation district rules is not to prohibit land uses."[28] With prohibition off the table, the state's role appears to be facilitation of development on ecologically rare and culturally significant lands, the prospect of which undermines the mandate of the Department of Land and Natural Resources to conserve *conservation lands*. Nevertheless, Hawai'i's Supreme Court rescinded the CDUP in 2015 because of the BLNR's failure to observe due process. In the court's opinion, Chief Justice Mark Recktenwald wrote, "Quite simply, the board put the cart before the horse when it issued the permit before the request for a contested case hearing was resolved and the hearing was held."[29]

Notwithstanding Hawai'i's often-progressive judicial actions, the alignment of state agencies, private capital, and big science suggests that the neoliberalization of governance in Hawai'i, coupled with the ideology of liberal multiculturalism, operationalizes settler colonialism. It also suggests that, far from defending the rights, sovereignty, or claims of Kanaka 'Ōiwi, legal discourse within multicultural society functions to contain them. Native culture, language, and histories are valued only insofar as they affirm the settler state's commitment to capital and its authority to govern. Also disturbing, though not surprising, is how the tension between its agencies and courts reveals the settler state's inability to resolve its inherent contradiction—that is, its commitment to both capitalism and Kanaka 'Ōiwi. In my interview with kumu hula, educator, and contested case petitioner Pua Case, I learned of the frustration she and her colleagues experienced in the struggle to protect Mauna a Wākea from future development. She expressed the pain of hearing University officials describe their concern for the mountain as a sacred site, a rare and fragile ecosystem, and cultural monument: "I think the parts that make me sad is when they say things about how they know the mountain is sacred to us, or important and significant. That they realize there is cultural significance and how much they love that mountain. And in the next breath [they say], 'But we're still going to build on it.' When you talk to two sides like that, that makes me sad because it's then I know that we still have a long way to go."[30] The disregard for the sense of injury experienced by Hawaiians caused by astronomy expansion on Mauna Kea is a reflection of the continued disavowal of American settler colonialism in Hawaiʻi more broadly.

Disavowal, Settler Colonialism, and Kanaka Indigeneity

Because Native Hawaiians continue to assert claims to lands expropriated from the Hawaiian Kingdom and a state sovereignty that never legally ended, Native activism, bodies, and desire for self-determination have become a constant foil to the state's neoliberal vision of Hawaiʻi. For this reason, the state endeavors to manage that opposition by fashioning Native claims as retrograde and irrelevant. One method has been to promote the touristic image of Hawaiʻi as an alluring visitor destination and racial melting pot, and to depict Hawaiians as a hospitable "host culture." The multicultural distortion obscures the historical grounds for sovereign claims by reducing Kanaka ʻŌiwi to a "minority" status. As Judy Rohrer notes, the racialization of indigeneity through U.S. law "renders indigenous claims inarticulable . . . while simultaneously normalizing white settler subjectivity by insisting on a color-blind ideology, an ideology based on ignoring historical and institutional white privilege."[31] In multiculturalism's strategic racialization of Indigenous land claims, Hawaiians are imagined as just another disadvantaged group vying for minority rights, one whose call for protection of historically situated Native rights becomes trivialized and recast as "special rights."[32] Any deviation from the roles to which Hawaiians are assigned poses a threat to the state's image within neoliberal modernity as capable of rational governance. For this reason, discrediting Kanaka indigeneity becomes a central concern of the state.

Consider a speech by former governor Neil Abercrombie delivered to the Kohala Chamber of Commerce in 2009. In his attempt to ease investor concerns in the face of Hawaiian opposition to the TMT, Abercrombie stated the project "will move forward. There will be no more obstruction from someone who found their cultural roots six minutes ago."[33] Here, Abercrombie dismisses Kanaka articulations of indigeneity and cultural praxis as invented and political as a means of affirming the state's commitment to neoliberal capital. In his 2014 state-of-the-state address, Abercrombie described Mauna Kea as "Hawaiʻi's gift to the world,"[34] echoing former University president M. R. C. Greenwood's 2011 UH announcement in which she also characterized the mountain as "a gift to all the people of Hawaiʻi."[35] As a discursive strategy this multicultural rhetoric is productive. It suggests Kanaka activism is irrational and opportunistic, while distorting Indigenous claims to land, nationhood, and sovereignty as excessive, reactionary, and aggressive rather than historically situated. A sense of settler victimhood is also suggested by the simultaneous vilification of Indigenous activism and recoding of contested lands as belonging to "all of Hawai'i's people." Multiculturalism succeeds in containing indigeneity by leveling difference, dehistoricizing context, and depoliticizing the social relations by which native-ness holds any distinct significance.

Differentiated "from other forms of colonialism" and by its "singular focus" on accumulating land, Audra Simpson explains, "colonialism survives in a settler form."[36] Patrick Wolfe argues that "territoriality is settler colonialism's specific, irreducible element."[37] Settlers are no transient visitors; they come for good. And unlike colonial forms in Africa and Asia, under settler colonization "invasion is a structure," not an event.[38] As a sustained process, an equally central objective is to deracinate Native inhabitants from these territories. Thus, at its core is a foundational logic of elimination.

However, elimination is only an objective, not an outcome, however close it may come in particular instances. Because Indigenous peoples remain and have the capacity to refuse inclusion, recognition, reconciliation, or displacement, Simpson adds, settler colonialism "fails at what it is supposed to do: eliminate Indigenous people; take all their land; absorb them into a white, property-owning body politic."[39] For as long as the Native continues to exist, settler claims to land and resources remain precarious, haunted by those they have dispossessed. This is its underlying paradox: any final realization of settler colonialism is inherently impossible. Elimination is always already a thwarted desire, despite its tenacity. Facing the presence of the Native subject repressed, settler possession and legitimacy must be made time and again. This explains the constant attacks on Indigenous communities around traditional practices and contemporary expressions of cultural identity, all of which challenge Native authenticity. Obsessed, the state endeavors to achieve its sense of right and belonging through dismissals and disavowals, carrying out practices of replacement through laws and techniques of governance that maintain socioeconomic, racial, and gender hierarchies.

Settler self-authorization does not always involve explicit displays of force. Indeed, in most contemporary instances it is produced within myriad banal legal mechanisms and the mundane, pragmatic bureaucracies that discipline Indigenous thought and bodies, and that structure anti-Native racisms and other social hierarchies.

As mentioned above, despite its theoretical utility for understanding this logic of elimination, settler colonialism can only ever be partial. Although it can impose great injury and pain on those it oppresses, settler colonialism is always incomplete and unresolved. Of course, for those who suffer from its hierarchies and violence, colonialism is not an historical anomaly or a system that was overcome by the multicultural state and capitalist democracy at the end of World War II or the United States' supposed toppling of imperialism. No, colonialism is alive and well, and it exists within foreign settlement and capitalist development on Indigenous lands. As Alyosha Goldstein puts it, "Settler colonialism in what is now the United States changes over time, shifting in disposition variously from accommodation to annihilation to inclusion of Indigenous peoples, while never being reducible to the encounter between 'settler' and 'Native' positionalities."[40] Even as it structures Indigenous subordination, settler colonialism is also inherently unsustainable, troubled by ruptures, exceptions, and limits to the power it wields over its subjects. Evidence abounds in the settler state's claims to legitimacy and jurisdiction over Hawai'i, which become less convincing with each iteration.[41] In these fissures there is a potential to transform those structures of dominance that control our mobility, thought, speech, bodies, and ability to determine the fate of our lands and waters. In these openings are windows to imagine other possible futures than those we are living. One central goal of Native and Indigenous studies scholars must be to pry open these rifts—it certainly has been for the grassroots activists willing to fight for the protection of the sacred mountain.

Gender, Tradition, and Modernity

Many critics of the movement to protect Mauna Kea ridiculed the kia'i for standing against the TMT in what has been viewed as a regressive and overly emotional reaction to something that is ultimately "all about jobs," education, science, or "coexistence." In these critiques, the use of coded language resonant with earlier colonial tropes points to the sense of American exceptionalism brought with the U.S. occupation of Hawai'i. Much of this rhetoric adheres to ideologies of white supremacy under the pretenses of economic security and scientific discovery. Anti-TMT activism is depicted as an attack on science, while basing that opposition in cultural forms of enviro-spirituality is equated with the anti-scientific dogmatism of biblical creationism.

Take for example a *New York Times* article by George Johnson, who claims that Hawaiian "religious fundamentalists" are among the last few left "still waging skirmishes against science."[42] His framing is predicated on the assumption that modern capitalist democracies alone have the capacity for rational thought as embodied in Western techno-science. His condescension to the land protectors, whom he describes as "turning back to the dark ages," builds on two presumptions. The first is Western science's triumph over tradition, superstition, and dogma, which has historically mistaken technological achievement with biological, cultural, and intellectual superiority.[43] The second is the notion of the mind/body distinction, which imagines modern man as overcoming the *trappings* of bodily desire and emotional weakness, both of which are associated with women.[44] I will tend to both. Johnson writes:

> This month a group of Native Hawaiians, playing drums and chanting, blocked the road to a construction site near the top of Mauna Kea and stopped the groundbreaking ceremony for the Thirty Meter Telescope. . . . But for the protesters, dressed in ceremonial robes and carrying palm fronds, T.M.T. has a different meaning: "too many telescopes." For them the mountain is a sacred place where the Sky Father and the Earth Mother coupled and gave birth to the Hawaiian people. They don't all mean that metaphorically. They consider the telescope—it will be the 14th on Mauna Kea—the latest insult to their gods. Push them too far, the demonstrators warned, and Mauna Kea, a volcano, will erupt in revenge. It can be difficult to tell how motivated such protests are by spiritual outrage and how much by politics. Opposition to the Mauna Kea observatories, which are run by scientists from 11 countries, has been going on for years and is tied inseparably with lingering hostility over colonization and the United States' annexation of Hawaii in the 19th century. The new telescope is a pawn in a long, losing game.[45]

It is difficult not to read these passages as the production of a new dogma where science and imperialism are indistinguishable. According to Johnson, Hawaiians simply lost. Native traditionalism lost to European Enlightenment and the inevitable march toward modernity—they should just get over it. Comments like these dismiss Indigenous expressions of pain, outrage, and resentment and recast them as retrograde impulse, reactionary, and irrational. However, as Glen Coulthard reminds us, "What implicitly gets interpreted by the state as Indigenous peoples' *ressentiment*—understood as an incapacitating inability or unwillingness to get over the past—is actually an entirely appropriate manifestation of our *resentment*: a politicized expression of Indigenous anger and outrage directed at a structural and symbolic violence that still structures our lives, our relations with others, and our relationships with land."[46] Johnson's rhetoric hustles to re-entrench settler legitimacy and white possession. It appeals to the underlying fears of white, masculine entitlement without explicitly naming it. Instead, he constructs a sense of settler victimhood, presumably caused by dangerous, angry, and irrational Natives. In my reading, Johnson does this through two specific steps. First, he suggests the TMT is a noble and universally beneficial project, "designed to see all the way back to the first glimmers of starlight" and representing "a triumph in astronomy's quest to understand the origin of everything."[47] Next, Johnson instructs us to understand anti-TMT activism as equivalent to an irrational opposition to science by invoking the seventeenth-century persecution of

Galileo. He writes, "These days the opposition [to science] comes not from the Vatican, which operates its own observatory, but from a people with very different religious beliefs. . . . It is not just religious fundamentalists who are still waging skirmishes against science." Johnson continues, writing that today it is "Indian creationists" who obstruct Western rational man's march toward progress. In other words, Johnson conflates the defense of Mauna Kea with the Roman Catholic Church's condemnation of Galileo for teaching the theory of heliocentrism. The fiction posits astronomers as victims and Kanaka land defenders as power-hungry Natives.

When Johnson claims Hawaiians have turned "back toward the dark ages," he is also enacting a gendered racial ideology grounded in Eurocentric conceptions of modernity. Arguably, his language is not overtly racist or misogynist, but the assumptions implied can be traced to the normative hierarchies that give modernity its meaning. He can associate Hawaiians with all the historical tropes of colonial conquest without recourse to explicitly racist or misogynist language, but instead through implication. Modern man coheres around white hetero-patriarchy but remains "haunted by specters of the feminine and the primitive."[48]

According to Catherine Scott, mid-twentieth-century modernization theorists' gendered constructions of "an idealized modernity" rationalized prevailing hierarchies structured in male dominance over women by disciplining subject formations available to them. To reinforce the idea of modern subjects and modernity's exiles, Scott argues, "constructions of traditional society . . . [mobilized] ideas about women, family, and community that function as points of contrast," against which the notion of the "rational, forward-looking, male-dominated public sphere" could be imagined.[49] Three major themes of these modernization theories stand out. The first is a "presentation of tradition as a bundle of characteristics that also have historically been used to subordinate women and denigrate the social relations associated with females, especially mothers."[50] The second is a "reliance on the public/private distinction in discussions of modernity and tradition," by which "modernity, rationality, technological progress, and good government are achieved in a public realm inhabited by autonomous men."[51] The third is the reliance on an "evolutionary model of social and political change" in which human development is portrayed as the "struggle for dominance over nature" and presented as analogous to male dominance over women.[52] The image of the unreasonable Native obsessed with tradition and fearful of progress invokes these mythologies of modernity that ultimately reproduces racialized and gendered hierarchies.

Sandra Harding also analyzes gendered temporalities embedded in Western notions of modernity, particularly as the category is staged in agonistic binary to tradition. She explains, "Objectivity, rationality, good method, real science, social progress, civilization—the excellence of these and other self-proclaimed modern achievements are all measured in terms of their distance from whatever is associated with the feminine and the primitive."[53] Harding describes how the modernity versus tradition binary posits women and Natives as inherently traditional and thus equally inferior to modern man. In TMT discourses, modernity is gendered masculine and associated with science, law, governance, rational thought, and the public sphere, while tradition is gendered feminine and associated with superstition, religion, family, emotion, and the home. When the binary is invoked, the result is not only the trivialization and discrediting of tradition but also the inversion of subjectivities, such that ʻŌiwi appear to transgress white possession and masculine authority.

For example, at the start of the protests in April 2015, UC Berkeley astronomy professor Sandra Faber sent an incendiary e-mail that was forwarded to a listserv of more than two hundred scientists. In that message Faber attempted to garner support for the project and to rally a counterprotest against the kiaʻi on the mountain. She did so by inciting fear:

> Dear Friends,
>   The Thirty-Meter Telescope is in trouble, attacked by a horde of native Hawaiians who are lying about the impact of the project on mountain and who are threatening the safety of TMT personnel. Government officials are supporting TMT's legality to proceed but not arresting any of the protestors who are blocking the road.[54]

Of course there were no "attacks," but Faber's sentiment points to the persistence of white supremacy in settler modernity. In her construction of settler victimhood, she neglects the history of violence by which Hawaiʻi was acquired by the United States as a white colonial possession. As if the political activities atop Mauna Kea exist in a historical vacuum, Faber, like Johnson, now represents the Native subject as a danger to not only the TMT project, but also civilization itself. Her rhetoric functions to remake settlers as "innocent subjects," Sherene Razack writes, "standing outside hierarchical social relations, who are not accountable for the past or implicated in the present."[55] The rush to innocence here resonates with the "new racial ideology" Eduardo Bonilla-Silva describes as "colorblind racism."[56] Any time Hawaiians stand up to settlers over the protection of sacred places or demand the return of land and resources through community demonstrations, we are said to be "overly emotional" or just "hung up" on the past. Where the expletives of earlier colonial racisms are no longer defensible, dismissals like these must be understood as expressions of multicultural racial ideology. It is a "racism without racists," the beauty of which, Bonilla-Silva writes, is that "it aids in the maintenance of white privilege without fanfare, without naming those who it subjects and those who it rewards."[57] It re-inscribes the predominant social order in which Indigenous communities are assigned to subordinate positions through the institutional structures that function to reproduce hetero-patriarchal white supremacy: "Shielded by color blindness, whites can express resentment toward minorities; criticize their morality, values, and work ethic; and even claim to be the victims of 'reverse racism.'"[58]

This racism resonates with that of Hiram Bingham, a nineteenth-century leader of the first mission to Hawai'i. He wrote, "The appearance of destitution, degradation, and barbarism, among the chattering, and almost naked savages . . . was appalling. Some of our number . . . turned away from the spectacle. Others with firmer nerve continued their gaze, but were ready to exclaim, 'Can these be human beings! How dark and comfortless their state of mind and heart! . . . Can such beings be civilized? Can they be Christianized?'"[59] Both Faber and Bingham's characterizations of Hawaiians dehumanize the Native subject as a path to self-authorization. When the images of the angry, militant Hawaiian or the ignorant, heathen savage are invoked today, the implication is not only that Hawaiians are immoral, irrational, and anti-science, but also that we are not even human at all.

In examining "genres of the human," Alexander Weheliye explains how "visual modalities of dehumanization" function to produce modern selfhood. Western society constructs a liberal humanist conception of man through racializing assemblages wherein "a conglomerate of sociopolitical relations . . . disciplines humanity into full humans, not-quite-humans, and nonhumans."[60] Examples can be found in early colonial encounters where the conflation of technological achievement and human worth functioned to expel the Native from the categories of rationality and civility. Constructions of modern man reinforce the inside from which the Native is expelled, signaling a threshold and outside to modernity.

Inclusion might seem to remedy the problem of exclusion; however, I argue the problem is not exclusion, but instead how settler subjecthood comes to signify humanity and draws the limits of modernity from which Kanaka 'Ōiwi are in permanent exile. The problem for Hawaiians is not one of access to the field of astronomy or the legal process, but how Western law, science, and the state together control the ways humanity is imagined in the first place.

A Fictive Kinship and Other Appropriations

The image of an obsolete, antimodern, and irrational Hawaiian resonates with two other, but interrelated stereotypes—the vanishing Indian and the uncivilized Native—which originate in the Doctrine of Discovery. As Roxanne Dunbar-Ortiz explains, "From the mid-fifteenth century to the mid-twentieth century, most of the non-European world was colonized under the Doctrine of Discovery, one of the first principles of international law Christian European monarchies promulgated to legitimize investigating, mapping, and claiming lands belonging to peoples outside Europe."[61] The work of the myth of discovery was to create a legal and moral justification around which to rationalize American conquest of Indigenous communities and settler colonization of Native lands. One effect has been to undermine and interrupt the thousands of years of Native presence on lands that precedes European colonization. This has been done, in part, by distorting the histories and cultures of Indigenous peoples through naming practices that rendered Euro-American settlement as the inevitable triumph of rational and scientific modernity over "savage" tradition.[62] Today, these discourses of civilization have become so taken for granted they are invoked in settler-colonial laws governing American Indians without explicit citation. They also proliferate in film, literature, and other popular cultural forms as if they are simply naming the historical truth of Native inferiority.[63] The persistence of these myths, as justification for theft of Indigenous lands and settler belonging, renders any grievance of Indigenous communities as anachronistic, unreasonable, and invalid.

In terms of U.S. governance over Indigenous communities in the nineteenth century, the Doctrine of Discovery was particularly effective in the "Marshall trilogy."[64] As Joanne Barker notes, the set of three pivotal Supreme Court decisions "provided the first substantive definition of sovereignty for American Indians by the U.S. judiciary and subsequently served to establish precedence for the trust relationship between the U.S. federal government and American Indian tribes (and, since 1972, Alaskan Native villages and, since 1920, Native Hawaiians)."[65] It is on the precedence of these U.S. court decisions and the racializing hierarchies they created that the state of Hawai'i's own trust relationship with Native Hawaiians is based. The Marshall trilogy formed the ground on which the fiction of white possession through "discovery" of Indigenous territories would be rationalized and "title" could be imagined. By invoking ideologies of civilization and enforcing its boundaries, American settlers also rendered Native peoples inferior and illegitimate. Like modernity, civilization has always been arbitrarily defined as an exclusive domain of Christian European peoples. According to the ideologies of discovery, civilization, and modernity, though tragic, Native death is inevitable.

Along with the collective indifference to Native genocide and the naturalization of white settler subjectivity it produces, today, multicultural settler society treats Indians as ungrievable. The logic suggests that because Indians lost, they should just get over it. Yet, even within those liberal multicultural spaces in which the "colonization and genocide of American Indians is a truth almost universally acknowledged," that violence is simultaneously "effaced and deferred."[66] As Jodi Byrd argues, "Indigenous peoples are located outside temporality and presence, even in the face of the very present and ongoing colonization of indigenous lands, resources, and lives."[67] The simultaneous presenting and absenting of Native peoples in law does not so much obscure histories of colonial violence as posit them to be irrelevant to contemporary claims to land and sovereignty. In these ways, liberal multiculturalism renders "indigenous peoples lamentable victims whose case is unactionable."[68] Within the teleologies of settler multiculturalism, land and memory are cleared of Natives, settler sovereignty is invented by settler laws, and Natives, though fascinating and unknowable figures, are little more than relics of the past.

In Hawai'i, these tropes loom over land use and Native rights issues. Kanaka 'Ōiwi are both necessary and necessarily a threat to settler society. Tourism needs Hawaiians, but only in a manageable form. The case of Mauna a Wākea and the TMT serves as a mirror of that ambivalence—a reflection of the simultaneous disavowal of Kanaka indigeneity and fetishization of Hawaiian bodies, culture, and language. Paradoxically, Hawaiians are a threat to settler coherence and a conduit through which settler legitimacy may be achieved. Just as the trope of the vanishing Native relegates American Indians to obsolescence and thereby clears space for settler belonging, discourses on "ancient Hawaiians" function to contain Kanaka indigeneity temporally, by confining their legitimacy to the past where it can affect neither contemporary land use decisions nor the myths of Native inferiority on which settler governance is based. As "archeological artifacts,"[69] Hawaiians may be celebrated as curios of the past in popular discourses, but rendered ineffectual because of their eviction from modernity.

Take, for example, an early Mauna Kea Master Plan summary in which former Keck Observatory directory Fredrick Chaffee was quoted saying, "After all, the ancient Hawaiians were among the first great astronomers, using the stars to guide them among the islands in the vast Pacific, centuries before anyone else had developed such skill. Long before Europeans and mainlanders, Hawaiian astronomers were studying the heavens with awe and wonder, the same feelings that draw modern astronomers to study the heavens. At this very deep level, I feel we are brothers and sisters."[70] Chaffee's statement imagines a fictive kinship that recodes dispossession as inheritance by inventing a temporal hierarchy that both racializes and genders difference. Through comparison with "modern astronomers," the move at once recognizes *and* trivializes Kanaka ʻŌiwi scientific achievements, rendered interesting but expired. The logic of this rhetoric imagines astronomers as heirs to Hawaiʻi and Mauna a Wākea by constructing a modernity within a linear temporality in which "ancient Hawaiians"—"long before" and "centuries" ago—are obsolete and thus inferior. As discussed above, the prevailing ethnocentrism of this view associates Hawaiians with the primitive and the feminine. These categories are antagonistic to a conception of modernity based on hierarchized binary forms wherein the Native subject is backward (vs. forward) looking, provincial (vs. worldly), narrow (vs. broad) minded, emotional (vs. intellectual), fearful (vs. embracing) of technology, impulsive (vs. contemplative), passive (vs. active), et cetera. This mythology of modernity rationalizes the hierarchies that underpin the settler social order and structure male dominance over women as a conditional logic of own possibility. Chaffee's ostensible celebration of ʻŌiwi scientific achievements, therefore, serves as a gloss to naturalize the idea of another telescope. However, in the process the move obscures the TMT's role in the ongoing colonization of Hawaiʻi. Here, Hawaiians are frozen in time—legitimate only insofar as we remain at odds with modernity. As Sherene Razack writes, "The definition of a successful settler project is when the indigenous population has been reduced to a 'manageable remnant.'"[71] The legal records, court briefs, witness testimonies, legislation, and derivative "official" discourses of the state collectively "tell the story of a pre-modern people encountering and losing out to a more advanced and superior race."[72] Thereby, "the settler and the settler state are both constituted as modern and exemplary in their efforts to assist Indigenous people's entry into modernity."[73] Settler subjectivity hinges on this relationship with Native peoples.

In another example, settler selfhood and belonging are again fashioned through a cultural appropriation mobilized through the episodes of speculative fiction. The same 2000 UH Master Plan summary features a quote by Hawaiʻi's monarch, Mōʻī David Laʻamea Kalākaua, in which he addresses a British expedition of astronomers dispatched to the Kingdom of Hawaiʻi to observe the rare transit of Venus in 1874. The Master Plan summary gives the impression that Kalākaua's support for the transit expedition indicates support for the TMT. In the document, titled "Voices and Visions of Mauna Kea," the Kalākaua quote reads as follows: "It will afford me unfeigned satisfaction if my kingdom can add its quota toward the successful accomplishment of the most important astronomical observation of the present century and assist, however humbly, the enlightened nations of the earth in these costly enterprises."[74] Recasting Kalākaua as an advocate of the project to expand industrial development on Mauna Kea today, over 130 years later, is a novel idea, but misleading. Far from anticipating contemporary ground-based astronomy and large-scale observatories on Mauna Kea, the objectives of the mission were rather modest. It was one of five British expeditions sent to different locations around the world to observe the transit of Venus across Earth's view of the sun, the data of which was to assist in the development of a more precise measurement of the scale of the solar system. Published in the *Pacific Commercial Advertiser* in 1874, the quote is from a letter in which Kalākaua welcomed the expedition, expressed genuine appreciation for their work, and offered the Kingdom's logistical support. Yet this context is absent in the Master Plan.

Kalākaua was encouraging not the development of telescopes on Mauna Kea, but the "costly enterprises to establish the basis of astronomical distances."[75] He was supporting four or five portable telescopes in Honolulu, none bigger than ten feet long, and all temporarily positioned for the single event. No permanent telescope was proposed for Mauna Kea. Yet the omission of reference to the transit of Venus serves as a contribution to the colonial rewriting of the history of sciences in Hawai'i. As Noenoe Silva explains, "Colonial historiography . . . does not simply rationalize the past and suppress the knowledge of the oppressed," it recasts that knowledge with ellipses, transpositions, and re-contextualizations to suit the historical narrative that affirms the requisite hegemony.[76]

The deployment of history to draw connections between earlier events and their relevance to issues today is not in and of itself a harmful practice. However, when the implication is made that Native historical figures, unable to speak for themselves, would support today's monumental techno-science on Mauna Kea, the discourse naturalizes the settler-colonial replacement of Kanaka 'Ōiwi by rationalizing the idea that settlers can also be heirs to the mountain, and to Hawai'i. No, Kanaka Maoli and astronomers are *not* "brothers and sisters" within this fictive kinship that imagines the expropriation of Indigenous lands and desecration of sacred sites as a destiny and desire of the Hawaiian people.

Our Worlds

In this article I have challenged settler framings of Kanaka indigeneity that cast protectionist activism against industrial development on sacred sites as antiscience, atavistic, and irrational. To do this, I have analyzed the reasons Hawaiians have put everything on the line to protect what is sacred within Indigenous thought worlds, onto-cosmologies, and cultural praxis. I have also interrogated the gendered and racialized hierarchies that underpin the ideologies of modernity and enforce a concept of humanity from which Kanaka ʻŌiwi are exiled.

So I return to the question: What can the struggle over Mauna a Wākea teach us about settler colonialism more broadly? In my view, Mauna a Wākea is about much more than just another telescope, the ability to observe the origins of the universe, the discovery of other worlds, progress, or prestige. At its core, Mauna a Wākea is about power. It is a struggle over meaning and its making; about asserting new relationships to the land, new criteria for legitimacy, new modes of belonging, and new meanings to be ascribed to the sacred, the natural, and what it is to be human. It is about the ways in which the settler state achieves cultural legitimacy from the ideological currency afforded to science as a voice of reason and providing a path toward universal truths about "our world." It is about the techniques of governance by which Kanaka ʻŌiwi claims to land, sovereignty, and independence remain in perpetual deferral. How are we to understand the controversy over Mauna a Wākea and the TMT if we fail to identify or accept the context in which this battle is being waged; if we fail to critically analyze settler-colonization under U.S. occupation? Indeed, contrary to statements frequently made by influential figures, many of whom are Kānaka Maoli and community leaders, there is no "getting past colonialism," particularly when it continues to structure our everyday lives.

To Kanaka ʻŌiwi the land is paramount because it is fundamental to our indigeneity. Indeed, Mauna a Wākea is more than just a list of physical attributes; it is our kin. As our kupuna are buried in the soil, our ancestors become the land that grows our food and the dust we breathe. Kanaka ʻŌiwi understand ourselves to be descendants and siblings of the land. As Ty Kāwika Tengan reminds us, while the bones of our ancestors are buried in "the same land that feeds [our] families and waits for [our] bones to be replanted by [our] descendants," we are birthed of the land in both a metaphorical and a material sense.[77] This is why Mauna a Wākea is sacred to ʻŌiwi. The knowledge of our genealogies, rooted in the land itself and linking us together as family, lies at the heart of our aloha ʻāina, our love for the land.

At the time of this writing, a second contested case hearing has just concluded after nearly five months. The kiaʻi fighting this battle within the legal space of the state are in an ambivalent position. On one hand, to stop the desecration of the mauna, our movement requires everyone to contribute to the struggle; no venue is irrelevant or inconsequential. So ʻŌiwi must continue to fight for the protection of our sacred sites, be it with our words in the courtroom or our bodies at thirteen thousand feet above sea level. Yet, on the other hand, in participating in forums controlled by the state and under the plenary power of the United States, a tacit concession is made, however complex and nuanced that decision may be. This fundamental bind is that to participate in the laws of the state is to recognize its authority over us. Yet, we cannot not participate, because to do so would only encourage continued desecration and industrial development of our ʻāina. I believe it is in such ambivalence that we find settler colonialism's ruptures, cracks, and fissures. In the contradictions of structured violence, Kanaka are unstoppable—though success is not always obvious or total. It is also the responsibility of every kiaʻi to exploit these ruptures, to pry them further open, and to thwart settler colonialism's ambition to replace Kanaka Maoli and eliminate our claims to independence, self-determination, and sovereignty.

The story of Mauna a Wākea is about so much more than telescopes and stars, science versus religion, or coexisting under the terms of the settler state. Indeed, Mauna a Wākea is a story about the future we imagine for ourselves and our ancestral homelands.

IOKEPA CASUMBAL-SALAZAR is a UCLA President's Postdoctoral Fellow.

Notes

1. I use the terms Mauna Kea and Mauna a Wākea interchangeably throughout this article. In reference to the Indigenous people of Hawaiʻi, I use Kanaka ʻŌiwi (Native), Kanaka Maoli (real people, i.e., Native), Native Hawaiian, and Hawaiian. Finally, for kanaka (person, people, Hawaiian, subject, population), I use kānaka for the plural (as with a countable number) and kanaka for the singular and the category, the generic.

2. See Patrick Wolfe, "Settler Colonialism and the Elimination of the Native," *Journal of Genocide Research* 8, no. 4 (2006): 387–409; Patrick Wolfe, *Settler Colonialism and the Transformation of Anthropology: The Politics and Poetics of an Ethnographic Event* (New York: Cassell, 1999).

3. Manulani Meyer, Director of Indigenous Education at University of Hawaiʻi—West Oʻahu, quoted in Lander and Puhipau, *Mauna Kea: Temple under Siege* (2006).

4. This point must be contextualized in the broader issue of federal recognition. In the last several years the U.S. Department of the Interior has been advocating for a process in which it would facilitate a "government-to-government relationship" between Native Hawaiians and the United States, a process that is touted as a best path toward restoring a degree of self-determination and protecting Hawaiian rights and entitlements. However, it has been hotly contested for its underlying ambition to seal a final land settlement and obtain the necessary, though currently unachieved, legal jurisdiction (i.e., title) over Hawaiʻi. Although such an examination is beyond the purposes of this article, suffice to say, the struggle over Mauna Kea and how the controversy is to be represented is best understood in the broader context of settler colonialism.

5. The heading above is a lyric from the mele hānau (birth chant) composed in 1813 for Kauikeaouli, the newborn son of Kamehameha I, titled "No Kalani ʻKauikeaouli Kamehameha III,'" also known as "Hānau a Hua Ka Lani" and "Mele Hānau no Kauikeaouli." It may be translated as "This is the royal offspring of night borne by Kea." See Mary Kawena Pukui and Alfons L. Korn, ed. and trans., *The Echo of Our Song* (Honolulu: University of Hawaiʻi Press, 1973), 12–28.

6. kuʻualoha hoʻomanawanui, *Voices of Fire: Reweaving the Literary Lei of Pele and Hiʻiaka* (Minneapolis: University of Minnesota Press, 2014); Noenoe K. Silva, *The Power of the Steel-Tipped Pen: Reconstructing Native Hawaiian Intellectual History* (Durham, N.C.: Duke University Press, 2017).

7. Noenoe K. Silva, *Aloha Betrayed: Native Hawaiian Resistance to American Colonialism* (Durham, N.C.: Duke University Press, 2004), 11.

8. Silva, *Power of the Steel-Tipped Pen*, 191.

9. See Mary Kawena Pukui, E. W. Haertig, and Catherine A. Lee, *Nānā I Ke Kumu (Look to The Source)*, vol. 2 (Honolulu: Hui Hānai, an Auxiliary of the Queen Liliʻuokalani Children's Center, 1972), 293–94.

10. This is according to the Lindsey family of Waimea as recorded by Kepā Maly. See Kepā Maly, *Mauna Kea Science Reserve and Hale Pōhaku Complex Development Plan Update: Oral History and consultation Study, and Archival Literature Research, Appendix E: Limited Overview of the Hawaiʻi Loa Traditions* (Honolulu: Prepared for Group 70 International, 1999), B-14.

11. Waiau is the only alpine lake in all of Oceania. Historically, to bathe in its fresh waters was an act of great significance for aliʻi (ruling monarchs) seeking the spiritual affirmation of one's right to rule as well as the mana (divine strength and mindfulness) to lead the Lāhui in a way that is pono (correct, upright, and in balance with the true condition of nature).

12. According to oral comments recorded by Kepā Maly given by panel participants Emma Kauhi, Leinaʻala Teves, Pua Kanahele, and Larry Kimura at UH-Hilo on December 1, 1998, "Mauna Kea and Mauna Loa are both considered to be kupuna; the first born, and are held in high esteem." See Maly, *Mauna Kea Science Reserve and Hale Pōhaku Complex Development Plan Update*, B-14.

13. Pukui, Haertig, and Lee, *Nānā I Ke Kumu*, 294.

14. Mary Kawena Pukui and Samuel H. Elbert, *Hawaiian Language Dictionary*, rev. ed. (Honolulu: University of Hawaiʻi Press, 1986), 169; Katrina-Ann R. Kapāʻanaokalāokeola Nākoa Oliveira, *Ancestral Places: Understanding Kanaka Geographies* (Corvallis: Oregon State University Press, 2014), 50–51.

15. There is some disagreement about the highest regions of the mauna, as some describe them as "wao akua" (a region believed to be inhabited only by spirits). See Pukui and Elbert, *Hawaiian Language Dictionary*, 382.

16. The Keck Observatory consists of twin telescopes with primary mirrors measuring ten meters in diameter, making them not only among the largest telescopes in the world, but also among the most productive.

17. General Lease No. S-4191. 2,033 acres were removed from the UH Management Areas and placed within the Mauna Kea Ice Age Natural Area Reserve in 1998. The lease now encompasses 11,288 acres of state land.

18. The "Mauna Kea Plan" was approved in 1977; however, far from a "management plan," this document addressed the technical aspects of research facilities and not the concerns of environmentalists or ʻŌiwi.

19. See the University of Hawaiʻi at Hilo, *Final Environmental Impact Statement, Vol. 1: Thirty Meter Telescope Project*, Island of Hawaiʻi (May 8, 2010).

20. Initially, only "native Hawaiians"—those of 50 percent blood quantum as defined in the Hawaiian Homes Commission Act of 1921—were covered under the Statehood Act. HHCA defines "native Hawaiian" as "any descendant of not less than one-half part of the blood of the races inhabiting the Hawaiian Islands previous to 1778." See U.S. Congress, 1921, House, *Hawaiian Homes Commission Act of July 9, 1921*, 67th Cong., 1st sess. C42, 42 Stat 108. Since the mid-1970s, "Native Hawaiian" began appearing in U.S. congressional legislation in reference to those whose blood quantum is below 50 percent. The Apology Resolution, signed into U.S. law by Bill Clinton in 1993, defines "Native Hawaiian" as "any individual who is a descendent of the aboriginal people who, prior to 1778, occupied and exercised sovereignty in the area that now constitutes the State of Hawaiʻi." The racialization of Kanaka ʻŌiwi into these two categories not only divides the community into those with access to homestead lands and those without; it also trivializes the significance of Kanaka indigeneity while normalizing the fiction that is the "State of Hawaiʻi." Today, the state Office of Hawaiian Affairs recognizes both "native Hawaiians" and "Native Hawaiians" as the aboriginal people of Hawaiʻi; the Department of Hawaiian Homelands continues to provide entitlements only to "native Hawaiians." In a 1959 referendum, the Territory of Hawaii was made a "state" when Hawaiʻi residents, predominantly non-Hawaiians, voted for "admission" into the American union. While the only other option to "statehood" was to remain a U.S. territory, many Kānaka ʻŌiwi refused to vote at all. Independence, self-determination, and decolonization were off the table, and justice deferred.

21. The term "ceded" is a misnomer, as control over these Crown and government lands was assumed following an attempted coup by this illegitimate group of traitors whose arrest of Queen Liliʻuokalani and removal of her cabinet were made possible only by the armed assistance of United States Naval Marines—who have not since left Hawaiʻi and continue to occupy the islands in violation of international law. See Tom Coffman, *Nation Within: The Story of America's Annexation of the Nation of Hawaiʻi* (Kāneʻohe, Hawaiʻi: Epicenter, 1999); and Jon M. Van Dyke, *Who Owns the Crown Lands of Hawaiʻi?* (Honolulu: University of Hawaiʻi Press, 2008); Keanu Sai, "The American Occupation of the Hawaiian Kingdom: Beginning the Transition from Occupied to Restored State" (Ph.D. diss., University of Hawaiʻi, 2008).

22. See Public Law 56-331, the Hawaiian Organic Act, April 30, 1900. Although the rich history of nineteenth-century activism falls outside the scope of this article, I will mention that it was Kanaka resistance which eventually blocked two attempts at a *legal* annexation of Hawaiʻi to the United States, a point I return to later in the article. As a result, the U.S. government passed the "Newland's Resolution," which was used to obscure that legal impossibility. As Keanu Sai argues, today's military occupation of Hawaiʻi and the act of Congress

on which it is based are violations of international and U.S. constitutional law. See Sai, "American Occupation of the Hawaiian Kingdom." In the interest of the stated objectives of this article, I have chosen not to provide a critical analysis of the implications of a strategic or ontological adherence to state-centered legal discourses as an means to end the U.S. occupation of Hawai'i or to achieve decolonization, although I believe such work is necessary.

23. See "An Act to Provide a Government for the Territory of Hawaii," Hawai'i State Legislature, April 30, 1900 (C 339, 31 Stat 141). For analysis of some of the effects of statehood on Hawaiians, see Haunani-Kay Trask, *From a Native Daughter: Colonialism and Sovereignty in Hawai'i*, rev. ed. (Honolulu: University of Hawai'i Press, 1999).

24. On the legal impossibility of U.S. jurisdiction in Hawai'i, see Sai, "American Occupation of the Hawaiian Kingdom." Sai explains how, without a treaty of annexation, the internal legal mechanism by which the United States asserts legal jurisdiction over the Hawaiian Kingdom is a legal fiction, despite its material consequences. Though it lies outside the scope of this article, it should also be noted the Hawaiian Kingdom was a recognized state within the League of Nations, the predecessor to the United Nations, evidenced by dozens of treaties with other states, including five with the United States and over ninety legations and consulates throughout the world.

25. For a particularly insightful collection of scholarship on this history of struggle and Indigenous resurgence, see Noelani Goodyear-Ka'ōpua, Ikaika Hussey, and Erin Kahunawaika'ala Wright, eds., *A Nation Rising: Hawaiian Movements for Life, Land, and Sovereignty* (Durham, N.C.: Duke University Press, 2014).

26. See Haunani-Kay Trask, "The Birth of the Modern Hawaiian Movement: Kalama Valley, O'ahu," *Hawaiian Journal of History* 21 (Honolulu: University of Hawai'i Press, 1987): 126–53, which surveys the events in a key period in grassroots Kanaka activism and political awakening involving mass protests against the eviction of families and farmers in east O'ahu's Kalama Valley, where a California-style suburban neighborhood was planned.

27. Office of the Auditor, State of Hawai'i, "Audit of the Management of Mauna Kea and the Mauna Kea Science Reserve," Summary Report No. 98-6 (1998), http://lrbhawaii.info/reports/legrpts/auditor/1998/scr109_97.pdf.

28. State of Hawai'i, Department of Land and Natural Resources, DLNR File No. HA-11-05, "Findings of Fact, Conclusions of Law and Decision and Order" (April 12, 2013), 92.

29. See SCAP-14-0000873 (Supreme Court of the State of Hawai'i, December 2, 2015).

30. Pua Case, interview by author on September 22, 2012, Waimea, Hawai'i.

31. Judy Rohrer, *Staking Claim: Settler Colonialism and Racialization in Hawai'i* (Tucson: University of Arizona Press, 2016), 107.

32. Such was the case in the U.S. Supreme Court ruling in the landmark *Rice v. Cayetano* case. See J. Kēhaulani Kauanui, *Hawaiian Blood: Colonialism and the Politics of Sovereignty and Indigeneity* (Durham, N.C.: Duke University Press, 2008); and Rohrer, *Staking Claim*.

33. *West Hawai'i Today*, April 1, 2012.

34. Neal Abercrombie, "2014 State of the State Address," http://dhhl.hawaii .gov/2014/01/21/gov-abercrombies-state-of-the-state-2014/.

35. "UH Update: Monthly Report from President M. R. C. Greenwood, UH System News," March 2011, http://www.hawaii.edu/offices/op/reports/march2011 .php?item=4.

36. Audra Simpson, *Mohawk Interruptus: Political Life across the Borders of Settler States* (Durham, N.C.: Duke University Press, 2014), 19, 7.

37. Wolfe, "Settler Colonialism and the Elimination of the Native," 388.

38. Ibid., 390.

39. Simpson, *Mohawk Interruptus*, 7–8.

40. Alyosha Goldstein, ed., *Formations of United States Colonialism* (Durham, N.C.: Duke University Press, 2014), 9.

41. Again, see Sai, "American Occupation of the Hawaiian Kingdom."

42. George Johnson, "Seeking Stars, Finding Creationism," *New York Times*, October 20, 2014.

43. See Dipesh Chakrabarty, *Provincializing Europe: Postcolonial Thought and Historical Difference* (Princeton, N.J.: Princeton University Press, 2000); Edward W. Said, *Culture and Imperialism* (New York: Vintage, 1994).

44. See Elizabeth V. Spelman, "Woman as Body: Ancient and Contemporary Views," *Feminist Studies* 8, no. 1 (1982): 109–31.

45. Johnson, "Seeking Stars, Finding Creationism."

46. Glen Sean Coulthard, *Red Skin, White Masks: Rejecting the Colonial Politics of Recognition* (Minneapolis: University of Minnesota Press, 2014), 109.

47. Johnson, "Seeking Stars, Finding Creationism."

48. Sandra Harding, *Sciences from Below: Feminisms, Postcolonialities, and Modernities* (Durham, N.C.: Duke University Press, 2011), 3.

49. Catherine V. Scott, "Tradition and Gender in Modernization Theory," in *The Postcolonial Science and Technology Studies Reader*, ed. Sandra Harding (Durham, N.C.: Duke University Press, 2011), 290.

50. Ibid.

51. Ibid., 291.

52. Ibid.

53. Harding, *Sciences from Below*, 3.

54. Janet Stemwedel, "Desirous of a Telescope, Team Science Struggles with the Practical Details of Sharing a World," *Storify*, 2015, https://storify.com /docfreeride/mauna-kea-and-the-thirty-meter-telescope-team.

55. Sherene H. Razack, *Looking White People in the Eye: Gender, Race, and Culture in Courtrooms and Classrooms* (Toronto: University of Toronto Press 1998), 10.

56. Eduardo Bonilla-Silva, *Racism without Racists: Colorblind Racism and the Persistence of Racial Inequality in the United States* (Lanham, Md.: Rowman & Littlefield, 2006), 2.

57. Ibid., 3–4.

58. Ibid., 4.

59. Hiram Bingham, *A Residence of Twenty-One Years in the Sandwich Islands:*

Or the Civil, Religious, and Political History of Those Islands (Hartford, Conn.: Hezekiah Huntington, 1848).

60. Alexander Weheliye, *Habeas Viscus: Racializing Assemblages, Biopolitics, and Black Feminist Theories of the Human* (Durham, N.C.: Duke University Press, 2014), 4.

61. Roxanne Dunbar-Ortiz, *An Indigenous Peoples' History of the United States* (Boston: Beacon Press, 2014) 199.

62. Jean M. O'Brien, *Firsting and Lasting: Writing Indians Out of Existence in New England* (Minneapolis: University of Minnesota Press, 2010).

63. For a discursive analysis of these tropes found in cinema, see Jacquelyn Kilpatrick, *Celluloid Indians: Native Americans and Film* (Lincoln: University of Nebraska Press, 1999).

64. These are *Johnson v. McIntosh* (1823), *Cherokee Nation v. Georgia* (1831), and *Worcester v. Georgia* (1832). See Joanne Barker, "For Whom Sovereignty Matters," in *Sovereignty Matters: Locations of Contestation and Possibility in Indigenous Struggles for Self-Determination*, ed. Joanne Barker (Lincoln: University of Nebraska Press, 2005), 1–32.

65. Ibid., 6.

66. Jodi A. Byrd, *Transit of Empire: Indigenous Critiques of Colonialism* (Minneapolis: University of Minnesota Press, 2011), 6.

67. Ibid., 6.

68. Ibid., 165.

69. Here I use Rohrer's characterization in *Staking Claim*.

70. Fredric Chaffee, quoted in University of Hawai'i, "Voices and Visions of Mauna Kea," Mauna Kea Science Reserve Master Plan and Implementation Process Summary (2000).

71. Sherene H. Razack, *Dying from Improvement: Inquests and Inquiries into Indigenous Deaths in Custody* (Toronto: University of Toronto Press, 2015), 5.

72. Ibid., 4.

73. Ibid., 6.

74. Kawika Kalākaua quoted in University of Hawai'i, "Voices and Visions of Mauna Kea," Mauna Kea Science Reserve Master Plan and Implementation Process Summary (2000).

75. *Pacific Commercial Advertiser*, September 19, 1874, quoted in Michael Chauvin, *Hōkūloa: The British 1874 Transit of Venus Expedition to Hawai'i* (Honolulu: Bishop Museum Press, 2004), 198–99.

76. Silva, *Aloha Betrayed*, 9.

77. Ty P. Kāwika Tengan, *Native Men Remade: Gender and Nation in Contemporary Hawai'i* (Durham, N.C.: Duke University Press, 2008), 25.

CLAUDIA B. HAAKE

Civilization, Law, and Customary Diplomacy: Arguments against Removal in Cherokee and Seneca Letters to the Federal Government

"**THE CHEROKEE PEOPLE** will never consent to sell their freedom—nor dispose of their heritage in the soil which moulders the bones of their ancestors."[1] This is what Cherokee chief John Ross and others, all part of a delegation for the tribe, wrote in April 1834 in a letter to secretary of war Lewis Cass. A little over three years after this letter was sent by the southeastern tribe, a group of Seneca chiefs from the Buffalo Creek reservation, part of the northeastern Haudenosaunee-Iroquois Confederacy, in one of their many communications to the president of the United States, expressed a similar reluctance to remove while seeking to explain their attachment to their land. They wrote that they had "resolved to adhere to our present locations to remain and lay our bones by the side of our forefathers."[2] While such a statement hinting at a traditional attachment to land through ancient burial sites was not all that unusual for the Senecas, it was one of the very rare instances where the Cherokee leadership in their communications with the federal government referred to something customary instead of focusing exclusively on their level of civilization or on their rights.[3]

In this article I will focus on letters, petitions, and memorials written to the federal government by the Senecas and by the Cherokees to oppose removal. Both had been formidable military and diplomatic powers in the colonial period, and both came to be threatened by removal at more or less the same time.[4] I will explain why, despite a shared focus on civilization and as well as on rights that both reflected the government discourse, there are also traces of customary practices in some of the letters, though more so among the Senecas than the Cherokees. I argue that the communications resulting from communal writing practices, even more and for longer among the Senecas than the Cherokees, reveal not only the oft-denied persistence of customary practices, but also constituted attempts on the part of the two tribes to persuade the government to reinitiate diplomatic relations with the U.S. government reminiscent of those of a bygone era.[5] As the literary scholar Christopher Teuton has indicated, to this day for Native Americans "orality continues to be invoked as a marker of authenticity," and the way tribes in the removal era were forced to engage with governmental discourses that were used to justify removal may well have contributed to the idea that some of them had surrendered their "Indianness."[6] Yet the letters analyzed here show that Cherokee and Seneca authors did not surrender anything, but rather used writing in defense of their own customs.[7]

Civilization and Law

In their fight against removal the Cherokees in their correspondence with the federal government used strategies that were not all that dissimilar from those employed by the Senecas, although the ways and the degree to which they were utilized by each tribe at times differed considerably. The most dominant of the arguments used in the letters were invocations of the degree of civilization already attained and appeals to rights or law, which was logical as these were discourses already dominant within the federal government.[8] When appealing to the level of civilization they had already reached, both tribes saw the need to provide some proof, generally in the form of material, educational, and moral advances made. They used these to argue that removal for them would be counterproductive, as it would not advance them toward civilization (as governmental rhetoric defined it).

The Senecas in their correspondence with the federal government repeatedly emphasized all advances made, be they material, educational, or moral. For instance, they stated that "our ancient hunting grounds have been changed into productive farms and thriving villages and cities."[9] They also pointed to having made rapid advances in civilization, morality, and religion, concluding that they were "not, like the western Indians, wanderers beyond the pale of civilization."[10] In contrast to this prevalent Seneca practice, the Cherokees provided very little tangible proof for the advances they had made toward what the United States referred to as civilization, at least not until 1836, when following the signing of the Treaty of New Echota the previous year—as well as the ineffectiveness of their legal appeals to Georgia encroachment—their approach to this issue changed to a certain degree. As the historians Theda Perdue and Michael Green have pointed out, they relied instead on their white supporters to mount such a case for them as the debate around the passage of the removal bill was dominated by Cherokee examples, and speakers in Congress often referred to advances made by the tribe.[11] According to the legal scholar Rennard Strickland, already "Thomas Jefferson [had] considered the Cherokee experiment something of a test case for all tribes," and the perceived importance of this tribe's progress is still obvious in congressional debates in the 1820s.[12] Unlike the Senecas, the Cherokees did not often mention moral advances. However, they ingeniously found ways to use even detrimental evidence to make a case for progress made in the realm of civilization in that sphere, at one point arguing that they were "now poisoned by the bad fruits of the civilized Tree," implying that advances made also brought vices such as alcohol as an unavoidable side effect, and thus hallmark of, civilization.[13]

Both tribes argued that removal would be counterproductive in terms of advancing them toward civilization. The Senecas wrote to the U.S. president that they believed "our comforts here are better than the Western territory can offer us" and pointed to the misery of white people who had already gone there.[14] If even white people struggled in the West, they implied, then Indians could not be expected to continue their progress there. The Senecas also argued that they could not go to the West as they needed civilized neighbors. Apart from thus contending that removal would be counterproductive by making them less, rather than more, civilized, these Haudenosaunee also maintained that they had "advanced to a point where we shall perish if we seek to return to the habits of our forefathers," thus reasoning that removal would likely be their doom.[15] The Cherokees similarly pointed to removal's likely detrimental consequences by referring to "those Tribes who have been removed from their lands," which were "now wandering over the wild and extended plains of the west."[16] They suggested that, if they were to remove, "their dispersion and ultimate extinction would inevitably follow."[17] Cherokee letter writers also feared that the lands available to them in the West "would not be adequate to afford us all comfortable residency," as in their estimation they were in "a remote a strange and a sterile region," concluding that "removal will be injuries wither [sic] in its immediate or remote consequences."[18]

The law was also something Senecas and Cherokees referenced when protesting against removal in their communications with the federal government. Both invoked their own laws as well as U.S. law. Within the realm of the latter, the Senecas repeatedly alleged bribery, fraud, intimidation, breach of treaty clauses, and other such legal infringements. They also took some of their grievances to U.S. courts, as—famously—did the Cherokees in what has come to be known as the Cherokee Nation cases.[19] And they, too, like the Senecas, appealed to treaties and asked for protection due them under the terms of such legal documents.

In the area of law and rights talk, which I take to be conversations in which the authors referred to, at times rather vaguely, U.S. as well as their own customary law, the Senecas mostly pointed to customary Iroquois law by invoking the need for consultations in open council and for general agreement. In their correspondence with the federal government, the Seneca authors also pointed to cases where those who had signed documents had had no authority to do so or lacked the necessary consent from the tribe that even chiefs required under Iroquois customary law. These were traditions that went back to the rules and protocols of the "forest diplomacy" of centuries past, which followed the principles of the Great Law of Peace of the Iroquois that laid down the rights and duties of chiefs, clans, and nations.[20] It stressed the proper way of doing things, as rituals and procedures were very important in regulating Iroquois life and society.[21] Forest diplomacy had been so important in diplomatic encounters of the colonial era that outsiders often had been obliged to adopt aspects of Haudenosaunee customary law, such as following the condolence ceremony before being able to enter into any kind of negotiation.[22] The Cherokees also repeatedly referenced their own laws when writing to the federal government. They mostly referred to laws they had adopted only relatively recently, as for instance the 1827 Constitution, many of which were modeled to varying extents on U.S. laws.[23] Still, some elements of these new laws harked back to or at least were not incompatible with older Cherokee customary laws, as for instance the lack of authority or consent they referred to in a number of letters. These references to their own laws and especially to issues about authority and consent, I argue, constituted an endeavor by the two tribes to make the federal government respect the laws of the Haudenosaunee and the Cherokees as equal to and equally as binding as those of the United States.[24]

Especially at the beginning of their removal crises it was not unrealistic of the Senecas or the Cherokees to expect some respect for their laws and legal system in U.S. government circles. The legal scholar Lisa Ford, using examples from the state of Georgia and New South Wales, argues that the extension of jurisdiction over Indigenous peoples by Anglophone settler polities happened between 1822 and 1847, at roughly the same time as the removal crises discussed here.[25] Prior to this extension of jurisdiction, the United States and tribal legal systems had existed side by side.

For the Iroquois this parallel existence of U.S. and indigenous law would have been illustrated by the case of Tommy Jemmy in the decade prior to the passage of the Indian Removal Act. In response to an 1822 charge of murder against Seneca chief Tommy Jemmy for having executed a Seneca woman convicted as a witch, New York State passed a law claiming jurisdiction over all crimes within its borders, thus denying the Senecas' assertion of sovereignty. Yet the legislature also opted to pardon Jemmy and thereby avoided antagonizing the Iroquois further.[26] It thus managed to walk a fine line, which seemed to suggest at least a limited respect for the Iroquois' legal system, at least for matters internal to the tribe. The situation regarding respect for their laws was similar for the Cherokees, which is illustrated by an episode of frontier violence and its aftermath.[27] On February 21, 1830, a frontier magistrate wrote to Georgia governor George Gilmer, informing him of an "arrest" of four Cherokees, one of whom was subsequently beaten to death. The Cherokee men in question had, on direction by Cherokee leadership, burned down settler cabins on Cherokee lands and had then been arrested by squatters. This arrest, the magistrate argued, was done under Georgia's jurisdiction, even though all the events had taken place on Cherokee lands. Earlier on, the federal government had refused to remove squatters from Cherokee lands and had directed the Cherokees to do it themselves, something they attempted to accomplish through the burning of the squatters' cabins. The U.S. secretary of war, taking a position going against that outlined by the frontier magistrate, defended the Cherokees' right to remove squatters. Again, for the time being the Indian and the white legal system coexisted, though somewhat uneasily.[28] Such experiences may have suggested to Native American letter writers that there was some hope the United States would, however grudgingly, show at least some respect for their laws, especially as many of the violations raised in the letters were also internal to tribal law, such as signing treaties without proper authority or consent.

Native Customs

Apart from these deliberate attempts to gain respect for their laws, be it old or new ones, Senecas and Cherokees authors also referenced their own customs at other times in their communications with the federal government. In part this may have been an almost accidental consequence of the writing practices adopted (which I will investigate below), but I argue that the inclusion of such customary references was also a conscious attempt to seek respect for what the tribes themselves held dear.

Over the period of their removal crisis these Haudenosaunee continuously invoked aspects of customary diplomacy and practices. For instance, while in the majority of their removal-era correspondence especially the Seneca authors adopted a mostly "white" and "civilized" style of writing, at times they used traditional kinship terminology. Fictional kinship had been the basis of the League of the Iroquois, the organization that had made them such a force during the colonial era, and in that period kinship metaphors had also been one of the organizing principles of diplomatic interactions between Native Americans of the Northeast and Europeans.[29] The use of kinship forms of address continued throughout the long Seneca removal crisis, during which the letter writers used such forms of addressing their correspondents in about a quarter of the letters written to the federal government.[30] Instances of addressing someone, generally the president, as "father" or "great father" were often paired with appeals for paternalistic care and benevolence, standards of behavior derived from Iroquois customs. At times Senecas letter writers also cast themselves in the role of children in order to make a request for protection implicitly—for instance, when Seneca chiefs explained that they had "taken little steps leaning upon the strong arm of our Father" but were afraid that "our Great Father forgets how young his Seneca children are."[31] They thus asked for the patience expected from a father in Iroquois society, but which would also have been a familiar concept to those from other cultural backgrounds and especially so to Christians. Letter writers of the Confederacy sometimes also demonstrated an awareness of ideas of paternalism under U.S. Indian law. At times the Iroquois and the U.S. conceptions of paternalism overlapped. In an 1844 letter to president John Tyler Buffalo Creek chiefs and warriors addressed him as "Great Father" and implied how he was expected to behave in this role. But the authors also linked this role to their new legal status under the Supreme Court's *Cherokee v. Georgia* decision of 1831, which described the legal status of Native Americans vis-à-vis the United States as resembling that of wards to a guardian.[32] "The law," these Buffalo Creek residents wrote, "declares us to be in the condition of children, and we expected the indulgence and kindness due to that character, so long as we are not willfully in the wrong."[33] In this manner, the authors combined red and white ideas about paternalism and used them to plead for protection.

Combining old and new concepts like this was not all that unusual in Seneca letters. A few even paired the seemingly contradictory forms of kinship address with gestures toward the levels of civilization reached. Among these was one of the many from the Tonawanda chiefs of 1843, in which the authors addressed the president as "Dear Father, President of the United States," and in which they used "Dear Father" several times in a speech-like manner, while also providing examples and evidence for the advances toward civilization they had already made.[34] Indirectly casting themselves in the role of children like this may have constituted an appeal to the colonizers' assumption that the Iroquois were like children, and therefore a request from them would be treated with the corresponding kindness and patience, or it might have been merely a way the writers echoed the condescending use of kinship terms by white officials.[35]

In contrast to the Senecas and other members of the Confederacy, the Cherokees hardly ever made use of kinship terminology; moreover, most uses in communications with the federal government were by the Old Settlers, those Cherokees who had removed prior to the passage of the 1830 act. The main body of the Cherokees, led by educated men such as principal chief John Ross and in something of a departure from the conventions of the previous century, generally followed white conventions of letter writing and usually addressed their correspondent as "Sir" or "Dear Sir."[36] And in at least one of the cases, where an 1837 Cherokee memorial to the Senate and House of Representatives referred to the president as "father," this usage may have been born out of desperation following the Treaty of New Echota and the tribe's inability to prevent its ratification, and could thus be said to have understandably deviated from normal use in their official correspondence.[37]

The use of kinship forms of address was not the only element of traditional diplomacy the Senecas used in their communications with the federal government. The "retaining and retelling" of old agreements through the use of wampum, shell bead belts, or strings, which the Confederacy as well as others had formerly utilized in all treaty councils, was another such example of a customary element of forest diplomacy that, in modified form, was used by the Senecas in their letter writing.[38] Even during the colonial period wampum and letters seem to have been regarded by the Iroquois as having at least similar functions.[39] For the Haudenosaunee, wampum not only contained messages or recorded agreements but were also an instrument of diplomacy, as they could be physically grasped or refused. Wampum was a sacred substance as well as a valuable commodity, and this stressed that the speaker was not just talking for himself but had the support of others. It was also a mnemonic device that helped speakers to recall the details of an agreement. Wampum belts were brought out again and again over time, and this function of "retaining and retelling" of an agreement helped the accord to be remembered and honored through periodic reiteration. It was this function of wampum that the Senecas in some of their communications with the government incorporated in a novel manner.

The agreement to which Seneca letter writers most often referred in this manner was the 1794 Treaty of Canandaigua, which they saw as guaranteeing their territorial limits.[40] In their removal-era correspondence, the Senecas invoked this document to emphasize their continued commitment to its provisions in a manner reminiscent of the ways they might have talked about the colonial-era friendship agreement of the "covenant chain" that needed to be regularly maintained through "polishing," as for instance by gift giving, in order to retain its validity. During a council in 1840 an Allegany chief told the government representative present that they still held to the treaty made with the "Great Father" in Washington, which they maintained guaranteed their possession of their "lands as long as grass grows and water runs."[41] And in 1849 Tonawanda chiefs appealed to the treaties "by which the lands had been guaranteed to them forever."[42] In several of the letters they sent, Senecas also used a wampum-like approach when it came to providing an account of history.[43] This retelling formerly would have been conducted with the help of wampum belts, which were held up while past agreements and their history were recited in preparation for the renewal of such accords. In their removal era letters, which were in many ways substitutes for the diplomatic councils of the forest-diplomacy era, Seneca writers at times still followed older diplomatic customs. One such example was a letter sent by the president of the newly created Seneca Nation to secretary of the interior Thomas Ewing in November 1849, in which the recipient was addressed as "brother."[44] The letter's author also referred to the "Great Father the President" and "his red Children" while providing a speech-like retelling of the history of the interactions between the Iroquois and the United States.[45] Another such example of a letter fulfilling the role of wampum comes from an 1855 missive to commissioner of Indian Affairs George W. Manypenny from the Cattaraugus Senecas. In it the authors looked back on their history with white people and referred to the chain of friendship while also creating a speech-like pattern through stylized repetition, repeatedly asking its recipient to "Listen while the Senecas speak" and using "brother" to address him, almost as if they were facing the commissioner over a council fire.[46]

Just as was the case for the use of kinship terms, other customary elements in the Cherokee letters are rarer and generally much more difficult to discern than the ones found in Seneca correspondence. Still, Cherokee letter writers generally seem to have tried to adhere to the idea of "good talks," especially by avoiding any direct blame whenever possible.[47] Instead of focusing on past grievances, the Cherokees customarily aimed for the creation of friendship and peace and often retold the history of friendship or tried to assign any blame to a third party.[48] Following this practice, in letters they wrote to the federal government in order to ward off removal the eastern Cherokees often blamed the state of Georgia for any issues that plagued them or complained about Georgia's actions, like the drawing of illegal boundaries or harassment.[49] Avoiding all blame of the federal government, in February 1824 they wrote that Georgia could "have no reasonable plea against the Cherokee."[50] They also rather vaguely blamed "white men" for various grievances mentioned in their correspondence. One such example is a letter from the same month in which they gestured to "white men" and explained that the Cherokees had become "a prey, defrauded out of their lands, treated as an inferior being on account of their poverty and ignorance, they became associated with the lowest grade of society, from whom the habits of intemperance, debauchery, and all the vices of depredation, peculiar to that class, now by them soon imbibed, their lands having swept from under their feet by the ingenuity of the white man, and being left destitute of a home."[51] In this letter the authors looked back at "the situation of our ancestors for two Hundred years back," but, while they referred to carnage and blood, the letter writers did not attribute any blame for these.

While an alternative explanation for this avoidance of direct blame in many letters, petitions, or memorials by the Cherokee leadership could simply have been the authors' wish to avoid antagonizing the federal government by echoing U.S. rhetoric about inevitability and attributing their fate merely to the unfortunate doom of noble tribes. However, even on the relatively rare occasions when they did assign this institution some blame, they often did so only in a very circumspect way. For instance, in a letter from June 1834, John Ross and others accused agents of the federal government of attempting to discredit them. Yet they did so very cautiously, seemingly still trying to retain the good atmosphere that was a prerequisite of a "good talk." "We regret to be compelled to say," they wrote, "for some time since, we have perceived an inclination on the part of, at least some of them, the officers of the Govt. to discredit every statement whether made directly by the Cherokee people themselves or through their representatives."[52] This was a far cry from directly accusing the entire government or any of its members. Despite these efforts to generally and whenever possible avoid direct blame, there were some instances when the authors of the communications clearly found fault with agents of the federal government and when they said so in their correspondence. For instance, in 1834 the members of a Cherokee delegation wrote to Cass that they felt the objective behind the removal policy was to force the Cherokees beyond the borders of the United States.[53] This kind of direct approach was, however, not necessarily incompatible with the customary concepts of a "good talk." Traditionally contentious issues could have been raised among individuals in a private conversation rather than in a proper council, where the Cherokees were generally striving for a peaceful, nonconfrontational atmosphere.[54] A letter like this, from the members of a small delegation to an individual member of the federal government, could be regarded as such a form of private conversation.

Cherokee correspondence with the federal government also indicate the survival of some other customary diplomatic traditions, such as appeals for "pity." In Cherokee usage "pity" did not indicate any shame or inferiority to those one pleaded with, but even so the use of this trope, as Cynthia Cumfer has shown, had declined significantly even prior to the onset of the Cherokees' final removal crisis.[55] Nonetheless, appeals for pity can still be found in some of the Cherokee communications from the removal era, sometimes in the form of claims of poverty or feebleness that asked the correspondent to take pity on the tribe. For instance, in February 1824 a number of Cherokees wrote to secretary of war John C. Calhoun explaining that they had been cheated out of their lands due to their ignorance.[56] They once again indirectly asked for pity in 1834 by referring to their own feebleness.[57] And in 1838, when threatened with immediate removal, they wrote to president Martin Van Buren, casting themselves in a subordinate position when they "acknowledge[d] the power of the United States."[58] "We acknowledge our own feebleness," they said, "our only fortress is the justice of our cause."[59] These veiled appeals for pity were few and far between, possibly because any complaints about suffering—and hence such pleas—could potentially play into the hands of removal advocates. However, the mere existence of such appeals signals the often-concealed survival of some older diplomatic traditions, something the general focus on civilization in Cherokee communications has often masked.

The references to customary diplomacy as well as to law and civilization in Seneca communications are relatively constant over time and occur during the entire period that members of the Haudenosaunee sent letters, petitions, and memorials to the federal government in opposition to removal. However, in the correspondence by the Cherokees there is some change over time; furthermore, the focus on civilization becomes less strict and later on—with the signing of the Treaty of New Echota and the looming threat of forced removal—was at times paired with attempts to explain the tribe's attachment to land. In this late period in their communications they explained that the Cherokees would not consent to the sale of their freedom and that neither would they sell the land "which moulders the bones of their ancestors."[60] Cherokee letter writers also referred to "the birth places of his children & the graves of his ancestors" and generally, from about the mid-1830s, focused less strictly on civilization and even attempted to explain why they felt attached to their lands—something, one might think, the government would see as distinctly uncivilized.[61] The reasons for this change in Cherokee letters, petitions, and memorials and its consistency in the Senecas' correspondence can be found—at least in part—in their letter-writing practices.

Letter-Writing Practices

It appears that Senecas' communications were generally authored by groups of people, often in consultation with the tribe, and many times may have originated in councils, thus in a way taking the place of what formerly would have happened at or in connection with treaty councils. Authors of Seneca letters, petitions, and memorials to the federal government included aged traditionalists like Governor Blacksnake and white-educated men like future commissioner of Indian Affairs Ely S. Parker or Dartmouth graduate Maris B. Pierce, and this was part of the reason why Seneca communications featured a mix of the old and the new, of civilization and customary practices.[62] However, more than merely an accidental by-product of the way the communications were composed, I argue that this mixture of elements in their correspondence was also a sign of Haudenosaunee efforts to renew proper diplomatic

FIGURE 1. Ely S. Parker. Courtesy of the Buffalo History Museum, Buffalo, New York. Used by permission.

relations with the federal government and to find compromises, as they had been able to do during the colonial era and into the early republic. Aged members of the Confederacy such as Governor Blacksnake, who reportedly was instrumental in at least some of the strategizing, remembered the days of forest diplomacy and the power the Senecas wielded not just in negotiations but also in shaping the form that encounters with outsiders took.[63] And even younger men such as Parker or Pierce would have been raised with the stories and thus have gained an awareness of the past ways. A knowledge of their history of encounters with Europeans and Euro-Americans comes through strongly in Seneca communications to the federal government; however, as I have shown elsewhere, it is often linked to potentially traditional ways of referring to this history, such as in reminders about past treaties or agreements that are reminiscent of diplomatic practices formerly associated with the use of wampum.[64] Such knowledge and practices might have informed and subtly influenced even educated men who otherwise tried to deny traditional knowledge.[65] Cognizance of former practices and power relations along with the fact that at least in the realm of law things had only changed very recently explains the expectations invested by Seneca letter writers in their efforts, and also proves them to not have been as unrealistic as they may seem to us now. Therefore such knowledge, as much as the communal nature of letter writing among the Haudenosaunee, helped shape the form and the content

FIGURE 2. Portrait of Governor Blacksnake by John Phillips, 1845 (ACC 1970.89.182) from the collections of the Rochester Museum and Science Center, Rochester, New York.

of communications with the federal government.

While the Senecas wrote most of their letters, petitions, and memorials in opposition to removal jointly, for the Cherokees it was mostly a matter for the elite tribal leadership who tried to defend the tribe's traditionalist majority.[66] Like the Senecas the Cherokees asked for governmental respect, but the discourse they adopted was for so long shaped by the elite that it was a mostly political discourse, as the literary scholar Maureen Konkle has argued.[67] It focused mainly on what these men assumed the government wanted to hear; only when the council was forced from Georgia to Tennessee, and even more so when removal was looming after the Treaty of New Echota, did increased

FIGURE 3. Maris B. Pierce. Courtesy of the Buffalo History Museum, Buffalo, New York. Used by permission.

consultation of the tribe lead to the inclusion of some more customary elements into the communications with the federal government. Most Cherokee letters, petitions, and memorials in opposition to removal were written by tribal leaders or delegates on remit from tribes but without an additional consultation about the specific content or form of the communications they sent to the federal government. As part of their efforts at centralization, the Cherokee Nation had also begun to appoint emissaries who received instructions about a specific bill.[68] Many of the communications written in opposition to removal originated with such delegates, and not infrequently they were written while these delegations were in Washington and away from the other members of the tribe, unable to consult easily had they thought it necessary to do so. Such delegates, often well-educated "mixed bloods," were tasked by the traditionalist "full blood" majority of the tribe, many of whom did not speak or read English, with the defense of Cherokee territory and the avoidance of removal.[69] Those like John Ross did their best to defend and help the majority of the tribe, as leaders had traditionally done by representing a consensus, but did this in the way they deemed best.[70] This approach becomes evident in the communications written by individual leaders or small groups of delegates on behalf of the Cherokee Nation, which generally follow white letter-writing conventions and show little trace of Cherokee customs. However, from about the mid-1830s onward, as the pressure to remove increased, the majority of the tribe seems to have had more input in communications, and the more traditional-looking ones among these communications originated in councils. Once the traditionalist majority of the tribe had a more direct influence on the content of the correspondence, putatively "uncivilized" sentiments such as attempts to describe Cherokee attachment to the land came to be included in the communications. This confirms what scholars of Cherokee history have long suggested—namely, that more traditional Cherokee practices survived until this period than has sometimes been assumed, mainly based on the picture of a "civilized" people the Cherokee and white supporters painted during the removal era.[71] During that time, tribal leaders, as the historian Andrew Denson has pointed out, "created selective, idealized, and at times simply inaccurate pictures designed to support their political positions."[72]

In her impressive analysis of the writings of several Iroquois and Cherokee intellectuals, Konkle has argued that some of them tried to deny traditional knowledge.[73] However, as the above analysis has shown, at least at times some of the same men were unable or maybe even unwilling to exclude certain traditional content when the majority of their tribe demanded its inclusion. For both Senecas and Cherokees the analysis of their letters, petitions, and memorials to the federal government in opposition to removal shows that, contrary to their claims of having left their "savage" past behind to become more and more civilized, many customary practices and attitudes continued well into the removal era. Some of these practices, consciously or unconsciously, found their ways into the tribes' correspondence with the federal government. This led to a mixed rhetoric in which, on the one hand, Senecas and Cherokees argued that they had become very civilized and had knowledge of U.S. law, but, on the other hand, they also invoked their own laws and drew on older diplomatic customs. While to an extent such

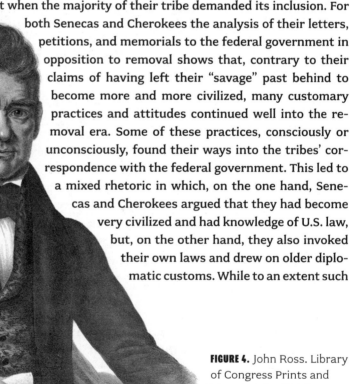

FIGURE 4. John Ross. Library of Congress Prints and Photographs Division, Washington, D.C.

FIGURE 5. George Lowrey, oil on canvas, framed: 29½ × 26¼ × 1⅝ in. (74.9 × 66.7 × 4.1 cm), GM 0126.2180, artist unknown. Gilcrease Museum, Tulsa, Oklahoma.

a mixture of old and new elements in the letters may have been caused by the letter-writing practices of the respective tribes, with the communal communications generally being the most traditional ones, it may also have been a conscious attempt by the authors to resume diplomatic negotiations with the U.S. government in a way reminiscent of the encounters of a bygone area. Seneca and Cherokee authors drew on the "civilized" skill of writing to defend some elements of their lives that would have been considered "uncivilized" by their correspondents within the federal government. The decision to embrace this civilized skill and even to engage with governmental discourses on removal was one taken up in defense of customary practices and thus cannot be seen as making Cherokees and Senecas less authentic.

CLAUDIA B. HAAKE is senior lecturer in the Department of History at La Trobe University in Melbourne, Australia.

Notes

I would like to thank Liz Read for her insightful comments on an earlier draft of this article. I also owe profound gratitude for their help and encouragement to the members of my research and writing group: David Henderson, Katie Holmes, Adrian Jones, Lee-Ann Monk, and Nadia Rhook.

1. Cherokee delegation to Lewis Cass, April 29, 1834, M234/76, National Archives and Records Administration of the United States, Washington, D.C. (NARA).

2. Buffalo Creek Seneca chiefs to the president, October 2, 1837, M234/583, NARA.

3. In addition to this, the Cherokees in their letters also focused on their nationhood. This aspect of their correspondence has already been impressively analyzed by Andrew Denson. See Denson, *Demanding the Cherokee Nation: Indian Autonomy and American Culture, 1830–1900* (Lincoln: University of Nebraska Press, 2004).

4. For reasons of space it was necessary to focus on communications in opposition to removal only. For an exploration of pro-removal communications see, for instance, Claudia B. Haake, "'In the same predicament as heretofore': Pro-Removal Arguments in Iroquois Letters in the 1830s and '40s," *Ethnohistory* 61, no. 1 (2014): 57–77. Memorials were at times written or cowritten by others, such as white attorneys. See Phillip H. Round, *Removable Type: Histories of the Book in Indian Country, 1663–1880* (Chapel Hill: University of North Carolina Press, 2010), 140ff.

5. For a similar argument but working with a very different body of evidence, see Robert A. Williams, Jr., *Linking Arms Together: American Indian Treaty Visions of Law and Peace, 1600–1800* (New York: Routledge, 1999).

6. Christopher B. Teuton, *Deep Waters: The Textual Continuum in American Indian Literature* (Lincoln: University of Nebraska Press, 2010), 11.

7. Rebecca Earle has called attention to a certain tentativeness about the use of letters as historical sources. See "Introduction: Letters, Writers, and the Historian," in *Epistolary Selves: Letters and Letter-Writers, 1600–1945*, ed. Rebecca Earle (Aldershot, U.K.: Ashgate, 1999), 3. Notable exceptions among the historians are Denson, *Demanding the Cherokee Nation*; and Nancy Shoemaker, *A Strange Likeness: Becoming Red and White in Eighteenth-Century North America* (Oxford, U.K.: Oxford University Press, 2004). Konstantin Dierks, *In My Power: Letter Writing and Communications in Early America* (Philadelphia: University of Pennsylvania Press, 2009) has also marginally engaged with Native American writing. Otherwise, while scholarship on unpublished, nonfiction Native American writing has increased in the last twenty or so years, the field is still dominated by literary scholars. These include Lisa Brooks, *The Common Pot: The Recovery of Native Space in the Northeast* (Minneapolis: University of Minnesota

Press, 2008); Hilary E. Wyss, *Writing Indians. Literacy, Christianity, and Native Community in Early America* (Amherst: University of Massachusetts Press, 2000); David Martinez, ed., *The American Indian Intellectual Tradition* (Ithaca, N.Y.: Cornell University Press, 2011); Maureen Konkle, *Writing Indian Nations: Native Intellectuals and the Politics of Historiography, 1827–1863* (Chapel Hill: University of North Carolina Press, 2004); Janice Schuetz, *Episodes in the Rhetoric of Government–Indian Relations* (Westport, Conn.: Praeger, 2002); David Murray, *Forked Tongues: Speech, Writing and Representations in North American Indian Texts* (London: Pinter, 1991); Laura J. Murray and Keren Rice, eds., *Talking on the Page: Editing Aboriginal Oral Texts* (Toronto: University of Toronto Press, 1999); Laura J. Murray, *To Do Good to My Indian Brethren: The Writings of Joseph Johnson, 1751–1776* (Amherst: University of Massachusetts Press, 1998); Drew Lopenzina, *Red Ink: Native Americans Picking up the Pen in the Colonial Period* (Albany: State University of New York Press, 2012); Lisa Phillips, "Unexpected Languages: Multilingualism and Contact in Eighteenth- and Nineteenth-Century North America," *American Indian Culture and Research Journal* 35, no. 2 (2011): 19–41; Bernd C. Peyer, ed., *The Elders Wrote: An Anthology of Early Prose by North American Indians, 1768–1931* (Berlin: Dietrich Reimer Verlag, 1982); Bernd C. Peyer, *The Thinking Indian: Native American Writers, 1850s–1920s* (Frankfurt: Peter Lang, 2007). Scholars who have made important contributions to other types of Native American writing include and Robert Warrior and Phillip Round.

8. See Andrew Jackson, "First Annual Address to Congress," *The American Presidency Project*, December 8, 1829, http://www.presidency.ucsb.edu/ws/?pid=29471.

9. Ely S. Parker, (identifying as) head chief and representative of the Six Nations, to commissioner of Indian Affairs George Manypenny, July 18, 1853, M234/588, NARA.

10. Israel Jimeson, Seneca White, and others of Cattaraugus to Robert H. Shankland, subagent for the New York Indians, September 29, 1848, M234/587, NARA.

11. See Theda Perdue and Michael D. Green, *The Cherokee Nation and the Trail of Tears* (New York: Viking, 2007), xiv, 66. See also, for instance, the speeches by Theodore Frelinghuysen, senator from New Jersey, or Henry R. Storrs, representative from New York, in *Speeches on the Passage of the Bill for the Removal of the Indians, Delivered in the Congress of the United States, April and May, 1830* (1830; repr., Millwood, N.Y.: Kraus, 1973).

12. Rennard Strickland, *Fire and the Spirits: Cherokee Law from Clan to Court* (Norman: University of Oklahoma Press, 1975), xiii.

13. Various Cherokees to secretary of war John C. Calhoun, February 11, 1824, M234/71, NARA. For more on Cherokee attitudes to alcohol see Izumi Ishii, *Bad Fruits of the Civilized Tree: Alcohol and the Sovereignty of the Cherokee Nation* (Lincoln: University of Nebraska Press, 2008).

14. Buffalo Creek Seneca chiefs to the president, October 2, 1837, M234/583, NARA.

15. Chiefs and head men of Tonawanda Band of Seneca Nation of Indians to commissioner of Indian Affairs Orlando Brown, June 23, 1849, M234/588, NARA.

16. Cherokee delegation (John Ross, George Lowrey, Elijah Hicks) to president John Q. Adams, March 12, 1825, M234/71, NARA.

17. Ibid.

18. Cherokee delegation (John Ross, R. Taylor, In. F. Baldridge, Joseph Vann) to Lewis Cass, February 14, 1833, M234/75, NARA; and Cherokee memorial to Senate and House of Representatives, February 22, 1837, M234/81, NARA.

19. *Cherokee Nation v. Georgia* (1831) and *Worcester v. Georgia* (1832) both were born out of Cherokee attempts to avoid removal, but especially the former has had an enduring impact on American Indian law by declaring Native tribes to be "domestic dependent nations." Many scholars have written about these cases. See, among others, Lindsay G. Robertson, *Conquest by Law: How the Discovery of America Dispossessed Indigenous Peoples of Their Land* (Oxford, U.K.: Oxford University Press, 2005); Tim Alan Garrison, *The Legal Ideology of Removal: The Southern Judiciary and the Sovereignty of Native American Nations* (Athens: University of Georgia Press, 2002); Jill Norgren, *The Cherokee Cases: The Confrontation of Law and Politics* (New York, McGraw-Hill, 1996); David E. Wilkins, *American Indian Sovereignty and the Supreme Court: The Masking of Justice* (Austin: University of Texas Press, 1997); Patrick Wolfe, "Against the Intentional Fallacy: Legocentrism and Continuity in the Rhetoric of Indian Dispossession," *American Indian Culture and Research Journal* 36, no. 1 (2012): 1–46.

20. See William N. Fenton, *The Great Law and the Longhouse: A Political History of the Iroquois Confederacy* (Norman: University of Oklahoma Press, 1998), 299. Others who have used the term include historians such Francis Jennings, James Merrell, and Daniel Richter.

21. See Fenton, *Great Law and the Longhouse*, 33. See also Anthony F. C. Wallace, "Origins of the Longhouse Religion," in *Handbook of North American Indians, Volume 15: Northeast*, ed. Bruce G. Trigger (Washington, D.C.: Smithsonian Institution, 1978), 65.

22. For more on Iroquois diplomacy in the colonial era, see Timothy J. Shannon, *Iroquois Diplomacy on the Early American Frontier* (New York: Penguin, 2008).

23. As several scholars have pointed out, one should not overestimate the change that the new laws brought. For instance, the Cherokee legal system was independent of the clans only in the realm of international law. See John Phillip Reid, *A Law of Blood: The Primitive Law of the Cherokee Nation* (DeKalb: Northern Illinois University Press, 2006), 234; or Strickland, *Fire and the Spirits*, 183.

24. See Claudia B. Haake, "Iroquois Use of Customary and United States Law in Opposition to Removal, 1830–1860," *American Indian Culture and Research Journal* 36, no. 4 (2012): 29–56.

25. Lisa Ford, *Settler Sovereignty: Jurisdiction and Indigenous People in America and Australia, 1788–1836* (Cambridge, U.K.: Cambridge University Press, 2010).

26. The subsequent *Cherokee Nation* and *Worcester* decisions by Chief Justice Marshall implicitly rejected New York's 1822 legislation as unconstitutional, but in practice this mattered little.

27. Ford, *Settler Sovereignty*, 131.

28. None of the squatters involved was brought to trial for the violence they had perpetrated against the Cherokees.

29. See Fenton, *Great Law and the Longhouse*, 29.

30. William N. Fenton, "Structure, Continuity, and Change in the Process of Iroquois Treaty Making," in *The History and Culture of Iroquois Diplomacy: An Interdisciplinary Guide to the Treaties of the Six Nations and their League*, ed. Francis Jennings et al. (Syracuse, N.Y.: Syracuse University Press, 1985), 21. This number, coming out of my own research, refers to the more substantial letters sent, excluding for instance very short missives merely inquiring about delayed annuities.

31. Seneca chiefs to president James K. Polk, January 25, 1849, M234/587, NARA.

32. Buffalo Creek chief and warriors to president John Tyler, May 23, 1844, M234/585, NARA.

33. Ibid.

34. Tonawanda chiefs, including John Blacksmith, to president John Tyler, July 12, 1843, M234/585, NARA.

35. Claudia B. Haake, "Appeals to Civilization and Lost Middle Grounds: Iroquois Letters Written during the Removal Crisis," *Wicazo Sa Review* 30, no. 2 (2015): 100–128.

36. Cynthia Cumfer, *Separate Peoples, One Land: The Minds of Cherokees, Blacks, and Whites on the Tennessee Frontier* (Chapel Hill: University of North Carolina Press, 2007), 25.

37. Cherokee memorial to Senate and House of Representatives, February 22, 1837, M234/81, NARA. The only other example of the use of "father" in Cherokee correspondence with the federal government is a letter from May 3, 1834, to secretary of war Lewis Cass, M234/75, NARA.

38. Wampum was used from seventeenth to the eighteenth century as currency in trade and for negotiations. See, for instance, Fenton, *Great Law and the Longhouse*, 7.

39. See ibid., 638. See also James H. Merrell, *Into the American Woods: Negotiators on the Pennsylvania Frontier* (New York: Norton, 1999), 193, 197. A Pennsylvanian present at the Treaty of Canandaigua conference brought beribboned messages along, presumably because he knew of the high regard in which they were held. See Daniel K. Richter, "The States, the United States, and the Canandaigua Treaty," in *Treaty of Canandaigua, 1794: 200 Years of Treaty Relations between the Iroquois Confederacy and the United States*, ed. G. Peter Jemison and Anna M. Schein (Santa Fe, N.M.: Clear Light, 2000), 76.

40. See Laurence M. Hauptman, *The Iroquois and the New Deal* (Syracuse, N.Y.: Syracuse University Press, 1981), 3ff.

41. William Patterson, meeting on November 3 with Allegany chiefs, in William Devereux to commissioner of Indian Affairs Hartley Crawford, n.d. [1840], M234/584, NARA. For instance, Pickering used phrase "as long as the sun shone" in his speech but not in the actual treaty. See Fenton, *Great Law and the Longhouse*, 672.

42. John Blacksmith, Jemmy Johnson, and others of Tonawanda to commissioner of Indian Affairs Orlando Brown, June 23, 1849, M234/587, NARA. See also Laurence Hauptman, *The Tonawanda Senecas' Heroic Battle against Removal: Conservative Activist Indians* (Albany: State University of New York Press, 2011), 31, 39, 66.

43. See Konkle, *Writing Indian Nations*, 231. See also Shoemaker, *A Strange Likeness*, 71.

44. A split occurred among the Senecas in 1848 when those resident on Cattaraugus and Allegany modified the traditional system of government by establishing an administration patterned after that of New York State. They changed their governing laws by adopting a constitution with elected leaders and a tripartite governing structure, and thereafter became known as the Seneca Nation.

45. S. W. MacLane, president of Seneca Nation, to secretary of the interior Thomas Ewing, November 7, 1849, M234/587, NARA.

46. Joshua Turkey and others to commissioner of Indian Affairs George W. Manypenny, February 19, 1855, M234/588, NARA. See also Michael K. Foster, *From the Earth to Beyond the Sky: An Ethnographic Approach to Four Longhouse Iroquois Speech Events* (Ottawa: National Museum of Canada, 1974), 206.

47. See Cumfer, *Separate Peoples, One Land*, 29.

48. Ibid., 28.

49. See, for instance, Lewis Ross and others, representatives, to secretary of war John Eaton, November 4, 1829, M234/73, NARA.

50. Various Cherokees to secretary of war John C. Calhoun, February 11, 1824, M234/71, NARA.

51. Ibid.

52. John Ross and others to secretary of war Lewis Cass, June 16, 1834, M234/75, NARA.

53. Cherokee delegation (Ross et al.) to secretary of war Lewis Cass, April 29, 1834, M234/76, NARA.

54. See Cumfer, *Separate Peoples, One Land*, 33.

55. Ibid., 84. For more on the importance of the atmosphere for talks see Reid, *Law of Blood*, 206.

56. See various Cherokees to Secretary of War John C. Calhoun, February 11, 1824, M234/71, NARA.

57. Cherokee delegation (John Ross et al.) to unnamed president, March 28, 1834, M234/76, NARA.

58. Memorial "by fifteen thousand, six hundred and sixty-five of the Cherokee People—as will appear by referring to the original submitted to the Senate" to president Martin Van Buren, April 13, 1838, M234/82, NARA.

59. Ibid.

60. Cherokee delegation to Lewis Cass, April 29, 1834, M234/76, NARA.

61. Cherokee memorial to Senate and House of Representatives, February 22, 1837, M234/81, NARA.

62. For more on some of these persons see Konkle, *Writing Indian Nations*; Thomas S. Abler, ed., *Chainbreaker: The Revolutionary War Memoirs of Governor Blacksnake as Told to Benjamin Williams* (Lincoln: University of Nebraska Press,

1989); L. G. Moses and Raymond Wilson, *Indian Lives: Essays on Nineteenth- and Twentieth-Century Native American Leaders* (Albuquerque: University of New Mexico Press, 1993); William H. Armstrong, *Warrior in Two Camps: Ely S. Parker, Union General and Seneca Chief* (New York: Syracuse University Press, 1978); Colin G. Calloway, *The Indian History of an American Institution: Native Americans and Dartmouth* (Hanover, N.H.: University Press of New England, 2010).

63. Memorial "To the N. York + Massachusetts Delegations in the Thirteenth Congress of U. States," n.d., HR30A-G7.2, NARA.

64. Haake, "Appeals to Civilization and Lost Middle Grounds."

65. Konkle, *Writing Indian Nations*, 256.

66. According to Cherokee understanding, leaders should represent a consensus. See Theda Perdue and Michael D. Green, *The Cherokee Removal: A Brief History with Documents* (Boston: Bedford, 2005), 23. While the literary scholar Phillip Round alleges that many memorials were written by lawyers, he also acknowledges that they mixed Native and non-Native discourse practices. See Round, *Removable Type*, 140–41.

67. Konkle, *Writing Indian Nations*, 46.

68. See Denson, *Demanding the Cherokee Nation*, 11.

69. Theda Perdue, "Race and Culture: Writing the Ethnohistory of the Early South," *Ethnohistory* 51, no. 4 (2004): 701–23. See also William G. McLoughlin, *Cherokee Renascence in the New Republic* (Princeton, N.J.: Princeton University Press, 1986), 170, 173, 238.

70. See Theda Perdue, ed., *Cherokee Editor: The Writings of Elias Boudinot* (Athens: University of Georgia Press, 1996), 33.

71. See Strickland, *Fire and the Spirits*, xi, Perdue and Green, *Cherokee Removal*, 13; Theda Perdue, "Clan and Court: Another Look at the Early Cherokee Republic," *American Indian Quarterly* 24, no. 4 (2000): 566, Konkle, *Writing Indian Nations*, 44.

72. Denson, *Demanding the Cherokee Nation*, 4.

73. Konkle, *Writing Indian Nations*, 256.

RANJAN DATTA *and* JEBUNNESSA CHAPOLA

Indigenous and Western Environmental Resource Management: A Learning Experience with the Laitu Khyeng Indigenous Community in the Chittagong Hill Tracts (CHT), Bangladesh

WE EXPLORE THE WAYS Indigenous identity and practice were framed in relation to the politics of environmental resource management.[1] We have examined two main questions: (1) How do Indigenous people of the Chittagong Hill Tracts (CHT) in Bangladesh view environmental resource management in relation to their own knowledge and practices? (2) And to what degree were governmental and transnational policies constructed within the contested social and ecological landscapes of the CHT? We applied interdisciplinary approaches in order to understand management in its relation to conceptions and practices, such as how to efficiently address Indigenous ecological, economic, and social challenges to those of us who have invoked this environmental resource management term. In accordance with the research questions specified above, this study was guided by the critical concerns of identifying problems of existing environmental management. Our focus related to everyday practices and traditional experiences within Indigenous regions. This study followed a relational research framing with an emphasis on the researcher's relational accountability and obligations to the study participants. We concluded by advocating for the Indigenous practice-based management for its effectiveness in guiding policy makers and researchers to develop robust governance for Indigenous knowledge integration in forest and land management.

The level of engagement in environmental management by Indigenous people has strengthened internationally. With an increase in awareness of their rights, their interests, and the value of their Indigenous sustainability, Indigenous people are appealing to offer their insights (Berkes 2004; Escobar 2010; Nadasdy 2011, 2003; Nakanura 2008). Considering environmental management as a component of complex social—ecological system dynamics, recent developments have identified that integrating traditional Indigenous practices, in addition to Western science, can increase system attributes associated with sustainability (Berkes 2004; Folke 2004; Walker and Salt 2006; Chapin III et al. 2010). Studies (Datta 2015; Gupta 2011, 2009; Escobar 2010;

Nadasdy 2011) also recognize that the Western and Indigenous meanings of "management" have fundamentally different perspectives. These interpretations stem from different worldviews with differentiated philosophies, practices, and methods. In many Indigenous communities, Western and Indigenous understandings of management are ontologically contradictory due to differing worldviews. However, some studies recognize the importance of Indigenous knowledge in environmental management with respect to implementing concrete policies at a local level. Currently, Indigenous management knowledge and practices have become an invaluable element of the Western management process (Berkes 2004; Escobar 2008; Gupta 2011; Nadasdy 2011). Amplifying attention on Indigenous practice-based management can provide further holistic understanding, with the potential to provide benefits for both Western and Indigenous sustainable management practices (Reo 2011). Such a shift could reduce misunderstandings regarding Indigenous environmental resource management perspectives, and lead to valuable insights for society at large (Tuck and McKenzie 2015).

Throughout this article, we recognize that sustainable management has many dimensions and meanings to the Indigenous community. We explored meanings of management through participatory action research (PAR) with members of the Laitu Khyeng[2] Indigenous community in the Chittagong Hill Tracts (CHT), Bangladesh. This community, isolated at one time yet thriving in its own unique way, is now on the brink of extinction (Adnan and Dastidar 2011).[3] Traditionally, the Laitu Khyeng took care when extracting environmental resources, prudent not to destroy the forest, as sustainability of their resources was necessary for their long-term survival in the area (Adnan 2004; Mohsin 2002; Roy 2000). However, according to Adnan (2004), Khyeng land-based rituals, practices, and traditional experiences, as well as the spiritually dominated sociopolitical structure, have been transforming in recent years. These changes, which have been reported in various research studies, are linked to government development projects and forest management policies. This can be interpreted as a part of new land-based processes introduced through the nineteenth, twentieth, and twenty-first centuries during European colonization (Adnan and Dastidar 2011; Mohsin 2002; Roy 2000). Despite the official end of colonization in 1947 across South Asia and in CHT Bangladesh, people have continued to experience threats to their land rights, culture, and spirituality by means of government land management, resettlement, displacement, development projects, and forest management policies (Thapa and Rasul 2006).

The focus of this article is to explore the meanings of "management" from Indigenous people's everyday lives and their natural resource embodiment. For this, we began by critically discussing the difference between the concept of Western and Indigenous environmental management. In addition, we discussed how we as researchers have understood and used the Western concept of "management" in our article. Furthermore, we discussed different agencies' management practices and challenges in the community that were relevant to this study. Moreover, we discussed our collective methodology and examined our procedures. We shared participants' traditional meanings of management from their everyday practices along with the participants' perceptions of the current challenges facing Western management in the community. In our discussion section, we have addressed why we, both as researchers and as educators, need to redefine the meanings of management from the community perspective and practices. Ultimately, Elders, knowledge-holders, and youth participants guided us with techniques to establish traditional knowledge-oriented management. This type of management can benefit both state and local communities in long-term sustainability.

Western and Indigenous Concepts of Management

The Western and Indigenous meanings of "management" fundamentally differ in terms of worldview, with their own philosophy, practices, and methods (Lertzman 2010; Lertzman and Vredenburg 2005). Dudgeon and Berkes (2003) suggest that the Western and Indigenous understandings of management in many Indigenous communities are ontologically contradicted for different worldviews, practices, and methods. Nadasdy (1999) and Simpson (2004) have shown that Western knowledge plays a superior role in environmental management, resulting in Indigenous management being delegitimized and ranked beneath science-based knowledge. Nadasdy (1999, 15) believes that the Western meaning of management "takes for granted existing power relations between aboriginal people and the state by assuming that traditional knowledge is simply a new form of 'data' to be incorporated into already existing management bureaucracies." First Nation scholars Battiste and Henderson (2000) suggest that attempts to define traditional ecological knowledge (i.e., management system) are inherently colonial, based on a Eurocentric need to categorize and control. Conversely, Indigenous methods of understanding management can be explained simply through Indigenous customs and traditions, their cultural practices, and the profound culture found in the cultivation and teachings of their land (Dudgeon and Berkes 2003). Similarly, Battiste and Henderson (2000) see Indigenous traditional knowledge (i.e., management) not as a mode or a component order, but rather for its great diversity as a reflection of ecological variance. There is not a universally accepted definition of "management" (Berkes 1999), nor is it a uniform concept to the Indigenous peoples (Battiste and Henderson 2000).

Indigenous comprehension of management can be used as a synonym for "traditional knowledge," one which recognizes that "traditions are not static, moreover they are continuously changing and evolving over time, as cultural groups innovate, borrow and acclimatize their [Indigenous people] traditions to ever changing circumstances" (Battiste and Henderson 2000, 75).

A number of Indigenous and non-Indigenous studies (Escobar 2010, 2008; Lertzman 2010; Bohensky and Maru 2011; Xu et al. 2006) recognize that Indigenous comprehension of management advances local people's ability to build their own environmental sustainability and elevates the importance of incorporating traditional management knowledge into policy and programs related to environmental management. Less attention is given by the state government to Indigenous knowledge in consideration of natural resource management in many Indigenous communities. Other studies (Briggs 2005; Roy 2000) of Indigenous communities suggest that we as teachers and researchers need to have a clear and concise understanding of the management of Indigenous cultivation culture, cultivation knowledge, and traditions while we are collaborating with Indigenous communities. Studies also suggest that Indigenous knowledge is not in opposition to Western knowledge, but is rather a knowledge bridge that can benefit both the Western and Indigenous perspectives. In this article we put forward the idea of building lasting connections of management concepts from the participants of Western and Indigenous perspectives. In the following section we discuss the differences of Western and Indigenous theories of management, and why we have used the Western concept of management with Indigenous meanings in our study.

Western Management

The notion of management in the neocolonial era has undergone little to no change from colonial perspectives. Although researchers have developed greater understanding of the importance and the role of Traditional Knowledge (TK) in environmental management, there is a lack of understanding from scientists, engineers, policy makers, and researchers about how to move forward with incorporating TK into environmental management while respecting the rightful knowledge-holders (Nadasdy 2011, 2003; Escobar 2008, 1995). Studies (Fletcher 2009; Lertzman 2010; Little Bear 2009) argue that Western management failing to honor Indigenous perspectives and to recognize them as significant could lead to economic inequality, displacement, loss of traditional lifestyles, and notable environmental damage to many of the Indigenous communities.

COLONIAL

Western environmental management not connected with local knowledge can be extremely challenging to the local communities (Briggs 2005; Nadasdy 1999). Escobar (1995, 13) explains that Western management knowledge, outside of local communities, is "exclusively reliant on one knowledge system, namely the accepted Western perspective. The dominance of this knowledge system has dictated the marginalization and disqualification of non-Western knowledge systems." Hence, Nadasdy (2003, 15) states that the Western meaning of management "takes for granted the existing power relations between aboriginal people and the state by assuming that Indigenous knowledge is simply a new form of 'data' to be incorporated into an already existing management bureaucracy." Battiste and Henderson (2000) take this even further, arguing that attempts to define environmental management systems in terms of Western knowledge are inherently colonial, based on a Eurocentric need to categorize and control.

ECONOMIC GAIN

Historically, Western forms of management have relied more heavily on outsider economic gain than the local people's needs, culture, and practice. These practices enforce profound, challenging, and potentially negative consequences to the local community's culture, knowledge, and traditions (Adnan 2004; Little Bear 2009). For example, Fletcher's (2009) ethnographic study of a southern Chile community demonstrates how Western forms of management have created serious challenges to the local community as outsiders have reaped lucrative benefits from the economic profit. In this study Fletcher discusses how outside environmental management strategies promote profitable policies by ignoring benefits to local people, culture, as well as management knowledge and practices. Therefore, Fletcher argues that the Western structures of management are a "cultural set of beliefs, values and assumptions that are active, implicitly propagated in the course of development" (271). Such neoliberal (Harvey 2005) management ideologies are interconnected with dynamic economic gains. For instance, Escobar (2008) illustrates that Western environmental management ideologies can promote material growth and capital accumulation; create a rational for scientific resource management over local knowledge; and emphasize privatization as well as individual economic gain and endorse commodification of natural resources. He argues that such Western management tendencies of economic gain not only create challenges for the local people and their traditional knowledge of management but wreak havoc on local practices and have serious negative consequences for local sustainable food sources, sustainable environmental practices, and local ecosystems.

PROCESSES OF EXCLUSION

Exclusion of local people and their knowledge in Western management creates a lack of trust for many countries (Escobar 2010). One study in particular demonstrates that the problem of exclusion is becoming detrimental in the continuation of power imbalances between the state and Indigenous governance. Wright and White (2012) claim that exclusion of local people's management knowledge in Western management leads to multiple problems for the local people, ultimately leaving the local people feeling separated from the process of management.

SUBALTERNITY

Western management processes create a subaltern group. For instance, studies show (Berkes 1999; Fletcher 2009; Lertzman 2010) that with the Western forms of management processes local people become subaltern in their land. We used the term "subaltern" according to Young (2003), which refers to a member of lower classes and social groups who are at the margins of society. According to Young, "subaltern" refers to a person without human agency. Within Western state management, management processes from stakeholders cause local people to become politically, geographically, and socially outside the hegemonic power structures of the colony and colonial homeland (Spivak 2006). Therefore, studies from the South Asian Indigenous scholars Chakma (2010) and Roy (2000) on Bangladeshi Indigenous communities illustrate how Bangladeshi management agencies (government, multinational corporations, and NGOs) justify state management projects over Indigenous people.

Indigenous Management

Indigenous knowledge regarding environmental management extends from a community-based and decentralized prioritization of resource management (Berkes 1999). Dudgeon and Berkes (2003) explain that Indigenous processes of understanding management are oriented according to Indigenous methods of interpreting, practicing, and cultivating culture on their land. Battiste and Henderson (2000) see in Indigenous management knowledge a great diversity that reflects ecological diversity. Indigenous interpretation of management has diverse implications for the local people. Various studies (Xu et al. 2006; Berkes 2004) explain significant Indigenous meanings of management.

LOCAL KNOWLEDGE

Local knowledge on environmental resource management is connected with local people's land, set of experiences, and the management of people living on that land. Local meanings are important to the local people, as local people have had a long, successful, and sustainable management history (Datta 2015). Gupta (2011) maintains that traditional knowledge is very functional and continues to be profoundly value-loaded and contingent on nonadaptive sociocultural features.

SACRED KNOWLEDGE

Land and environment management practices are sacred knowledge to the Indigenous people (Berkes 1999). The study by Xu and colleagues (2006) on southwestern China shows how Indigenous sacred management knowledge has contributed to the maintenance of cultural and biological diversity throughout many centuries in China. This knowledge may help improve the effectiveness of today's conservation policies by increasing their flexibility and local relevance. Xu and colleagues explain how sacred knowledge is extremely effective for the local people and for environmental management. The local people name each piece of land and each house on that land, and award the name of that house as a family name. The external world beyond the walls of the house consists of arable lands, grazing rangelands, and lakes and forests complemented by plants, trees, fish, and wildlife. Sacred objects such as incense-burning podiums, pagodas, and mini-stones function as special areas for the local community to share meaningful dialogue between life and spirits in the external world. The community believes that the environment is a scared place and that the spirits are their ultimate guide.

PRACTICAL KNOWLEDGE

Indigenous management knowledge, connected with people and everyday life, is constantly reinforced through experience. This experience is essentially the result of generations of intelligent reasoning. Article 8 of the Convention on Biological Diversity asserts that "respect, preservation and maintenance of knowledge innovation and practices of Indigenous and local communities who embody traditional lifestyles are relevant for the conservation and sustainable use of biological diversity" (United Nations 2013). Furthering this position, Gadgil, Berkes, and Folke (1993) explain that Indigenous environmental management knowledge has been rediscovered as a model for recognition of their land rights, identity, and interests—thus resulting in a healthy interaction and use of the environment in order to gain new perspectives on the relationship between humans and nature.

DIVERSE KNOWLEDGE

Indigenous knowledge is diverse and fluid in accordance to everyday practices with the land, animals, and other species (Datta et al. 2014). It is continuously changing, with no end in sight. Negotiation is a central concept for Indigenous management (Butler et al. 2012). Berkes (2012, 8) provides detailed explanations of Indigenous management as "a cumulative body of knowledge, practice and beliefs, evolving by adaptive processes and handed down through the generations by cultural transmission and towards the relationship of living things (including humans) with one another and with their environment."

SCIENTIFIC KNOWLEDGE

Indigenous management knowledge has been historically successful to a much larger degree than other forms of knowledge, including Western management (Lévi-Strauss 1968). Therefore, Indigenous people refer to their knowledge as scientific knowledge, which arises from its generational context of everyday production (Aikenhead and Ogawa 2007; Datta 2015).

SPIRITUAL KNOWLEDGE

Indigenous management knowledge is connected with everyday spirituality. In this spiritual process every animal, plant, and person is connected with one another (Latour 2004). The environment and people are not separate entities, and both have their own managing capacity. Management here is considered a spiritual relationship rather than one having more superiority over another (Gadgil, Berkes, and Folke 1993).

HOLISTIC KNOWLEDGE

Indigenous management knowledge is holistic, integrative, and situated within broader cultural traditions (Wilson 2008). It does not distinguish between technical/nontechnical, rational/nonrational, and science/culture (Lertzman 2010). While Indigenous knowledge on environmental resource management may indeed be represented as a holistic and relevant alternative to Western science, Indigenous knowledge realistically needs to be seen as something more nuanced, pragmatic, and flexible, perhaps even provisional, negotiable, and dynamic (Briggs 2005).

Therefore, in our research we discussed differences between Western and Indigenous meanings of "management" at length with Elders, knowledge-holders, leaders, and co-researcher participants. We have agreed to use the term "management" according to the community's methods of understanding, practicing, and respecting their land, water, and environment (see Figure 1). Participants were interested in learning the Western concept of management, used significantly in the Bangladeshi state land and forest policies as well as internationally. For example, during a telephone conversation, Elder Basa Khyeng proclaimed, "We need to talk and use the words [management] as the Bangladeshi government uses it in order for our government and international agencies to understand the importance of our traditional cultivation practices." We had further discussions regarding Indigenous management knowledge and its potential outcome when integrated with Western science. We discussed how management knowledge would result in epistemological pluralism, potentially enhancing the resilience of social-ecological systems by providing a diversity of knowledge for problem solving (Berkes 1999; Briggs

FIGURE 1.
The top photo shows traditional jhum and plain land cultivation; the bottom photo shows how traditional knowledge was used to inform the development of a water treatment plant in the community.

and Sharp 2004). In defining how Indigenous ways of thinking can challenge Western knowledge, Briggs and Sharp (2004, 673) suggest that "Indigenous knowledge all over the world is malleable, conforming in response to Western ideas and practices." Similar studies (Berkes 2009; Bohensky and Maru 2011; Folke 2004) maintain that the understanding of Indigenous management can include land-based information, trust-building information, as well as management techniques and institutions.

We are not disputing the idea that all Western knowledge is problematic; we are simply sharing our knowledge taught from one of the CHT Indigenous communities on how Western management can be challenging to the local people if it is not stemming from and taught by the local people (Adnan 2004; Brosius 1997; Roy 2000). According to the teachings of our Elders and knowledge-holders, several in-depth telephone conversations, and the compilation of information from within our sharing circles, we have summarized that we can build strength and solidarity together, simply by honoring and sharing our knowledge and understanding, ultimately enriching both. It certainly is not one idea or concept over another, but rather a reciprocal manner of integrating ideas in order for the local people to benefit and to aid in the construction of building bridges (Briggs 2005). Therefore, the participants in our research believe that Indigenous peoples' meanings of management play significant roles connecting Western and Indigenous ways of knowing and acting, so long as the Indigenous meanings of management are a cumulative body of knowledge. This includes relational practices and belief systems that evolve by adaptive processes, incorporating traditions that have been handed down through the generations together with a strong understanding of cultural transmission about the relationships of all things (i.e., both human and nonhuman beings) with one another and with the environment (Berkes 2009; Latour 2004). Participants suggested that the community's understandings of land, water, and environmental management are interconnected with types of crops, cultivation tools, and domestic animals, traditional administrative, spirituality, and local markets.

Different Agencies' Management Practices and Challenges

Indigenous knowledge has been historically significant for CHT Indigenous communities' lives, identity, cultivation culture, and everyday practices (Adnan 2004). The CHT Indigenous scholar Roy (2000) suggests that such knowledge is a process of empowerment for Indigenous men and women on their land. Other Indigenous studies (Chakma 2010; Thapa and Rasul 2006) explored how Indigenous knowledge equally engages men/women and animals, as well as traditional native plants and landscape. It is also offers a process that sustains a rich biodiversity of plant varieties (Chakma, 2010). Indigenous land management practices however, have been challenged by the land management approaches of both the British colonial state (1757–1947) and neocolonial states (Pakistan, 1947–71; Bangladesh, 1972–present) (Adnan and Dastidar, 2011).

Government land management interventions in the CHT started during the British colonial period (Adnan 2004; Adnan and Dastidar 2011; Chakma 2010; Roy 2000). In 1882–83 the British colonial government first declared 24 percent of Indigenous land as a reserved forest, without consulting with the Indigenous people of the CHT (Roy 2000). Roy argues that the incorporation of traditional, local knowledge into environmental decision–making is an essential tool for working toward the improvement of Indigenous environmental sustainability. Similarly, addressing the ongoing effects of colonialism and decolonizing environmental decision making is inherently related to the improvement of Indigenous environmental sustainability. Roy shows ongoing effects of colonization. By the name of state's reserve forest, Indigenous land were stolen for the purpose of non-Indigenous economic profit. This form of colonization was implemented by the British colonial state starting in 1900. The British colonial state's land–management approaches were officially promoted through the British government's 1900 regulation (Rule 34). In the CHTs, the 1900 regulation had been widely criticized for increasing the local population. Thus, in the 1920s, the colonial state strictly forbade outsiders due to the significant increase of plain land population in the CHT (Adnan 2004).[4] Indigenous traditional land management and spiritual practices began to face significant challenges through British colonial policies.

Not only did colonial land management strategies in the CHT Indigenous land go unchallenged during the neocolonial Pakistani and Bangladeshi state regimes, but these strategies became another obstacle for Indigenous spiritual and relational land management practices (Adnan 2004; Mohsin 2002). According to Mohsin (1997) the Pakistani government sponsored a number of land management projects on CHT Indigenous land that resulted in land alienation, control of land rights, and changes in resource management. The Laitu Khyeng Indigenous community, like other Indigenous communities in the CHT, faced many challenges as a result of such Pakistani government management projects, including the Karnafuli Paper Mill in 1953, Kapati Dam between 1957 and 1963, and a change to Rule 34 by the Pakistan government (Adnan and Dastidar 2011). The Karnafuli Paper Mill was the first project of the Pakistani state government that prohibited Indigenous traditional cultivation and cutting of spiritual plants and trees from the Indigenous motherland. According to Adnan (2004), Roy (1998), and Mohsin (1997) the Pakistani government's most controversial land management project, the Kapati Dam, was undertaken on CHT Indigenous land. Adnan (2004) states that one of the main targets of this management project was to produce electricity for outsiders, with all the jobs in the construction phase offered to those outsiders. The project (also known as the Kapati Electric Dam) flooded 40 percent of the Indigenous cultivated land, displacing hundreds of thousands of Indigenous people. This led to slow population growth in the CHT area. Furthermore, according to Mohsin (2002) and Schendel and colleagues (2001), another significant threat to CHT Indigenous land management policies in the 1960s was the Pakistani government's redefining of Rule 34, which allowed the government to offer access to Indigenous land without Indigenous communities' consent. All three land management projects devastated the region and had disproportionately negative effects on Indigenous communities. In the Bangladeshi (1972 to present) the new settlement project started and hundred of thousands Indigenous people were removed from their land. This brought forth governmental incentives to new settlers in the Indigenous land by weekly food support in the name of protecting nationhood (Adnan 2004). During this time, under two political regimes, there were more than one hundred thousand internal migrations in the CHT by this management project (Adnan 2004; Roy 2000). Adnan and Dastidar (2011) state that this illegal migration is still continuing under various management projects. Under the neocolonial Bangladeshi state's land management policies, not only have traditional land-based practices been identified as "anti-development" but Indigenous traditional experiences have been recognized as "anti-national" ideas (Adnan and Dastidar 2011, 130). Indeed, various studies (e.g., Adnan 2004; Mohsin 2002; Roy 1998) show that Bangladeshi state land management projects have become more exploitative in order to justify forceful migration into Indigenous land, arguing that all land rights are owned by the government and not by the local Indigenous people.

Nongovernmental agencies (i.e., private rubber plantation companies, brickfields, British–American tobacco companies, oil and gas exploration companies, micro-credit businesses, and private lumber plantation companies) have been using CHT Indigenous land, forest, and water resources with the consent of CHT Indigenous communities while introducing large amounts of transmigration into the CHT (Adnan 2004; Chakma 2010). Adnan (2004, 122) argues that the management projects of nongovernmental agencies extracted "400 species of trees growing in the natural forests of the CHT." In his explanation of management impacts of nongovernmental agencies on Indigenous environmental sustainability, Adnan shows that outsiders (i.e., nongovernmental agencies) have enforced management strategies introduced to the Indigenous people that lead to "continuing environmental degradation, threatening its agricultural and forestry-based production including the livelihood of the inhabitants" (149). These are directly connected with "poverty, economic exploitation, forcible land occupation and political domination" within the CHT Indigenous communities (162).

Why Is This Study Significant?

This article infused various gaps of knowledge in the Laitu Khyeng Indigenous community of Bangladesh. In particular, this study explored Indigenous definitions of environmental management by means of examining Indigenous land alienation, the importance of local practices, and municipal methods of implementing sustainability. The study also investigated the concerns regarding existing governmental and nongovernmental land management projects. In accordance with the research questions, this study was measured by identifying critical concerns with respect to existing land management and policies. The study was also based on discovering strategies that framed the Laitu Khyeng Indigenous community's ideas of management as they related to their everyday land management practices and traditional experiences of management. This study positioned itself within this context and drew significant steps in exploring identity and justice in relation to Indigenous understandings of sustainability and land management (Adnan 2004; McKenzie et al. 2009).

The review aimed to contribute through research, alongside a process that would benefit the participants with the hopes of inspiring a new culture of sustainability within Indigenous regions, particularly in the Laitu Khyeng Indigenous community. As an example, participants articulated diverse cultural practices in relation to environmental issues and solutions. They demonstrated relationships with their environment and with their ancestral land and water, finding opportunities to document their traditional experiences with their environment.

Methodology

Using the conceptual framework of a relational ontology, we examined the meaning of management with a focus on traditional experiences, culture, and customs, which are all of considerable importance for Indigenous lives and the environment (Datta 2015). A relational ontology invokes a collaboration of ontologies that come from everyday culture and practices (Datta 2015; Escobar 2010). The conceptual framework deconstructs our preexisting ideas of land management and implicitly leaves behind all prioritization that contains a modern dualistic source (Datta et al. 2014). A relational ontology also focuses on the researcher's relational accountability and obligations to the study's participants and research site (Datta et al. 2014; Wilson 2008).

To complement a relational theoretical framework, we used a participatory action research methodology. PAR has been used to foster change through community-based participation (Datta et al. 2014). In PAR, five methods of data collection were used, including traditional sharing circles. These methods were used for sharing land management experiences and expectations within the community. Individual story sharing was applied for a deeper understanding of land management and sustainability from the participants' personal experiences. Photovoice was implemented in order to restore relational and spiritual land management stories. Commonplace books (Sumara 1996) were added for the collection of personal experiences and feelings regarding land management practices and how they were introduced. Finally, participant observation was used for understanding and interpreting the expression and responses of the participants. Our research engaged community Elders, knowledge holders, leaders, and youths. These processes, such as conducting research, data analysis, and identifying research theme results, encouraged critical thinking, acceptance of responsibilities, and building community-based sustainability (Datta 2015; Datta et al. 2014; Wilson 2008).

The Community's Views on Traditional Management

An important concern that continued to arise throughout our research was the issue of knowledge and practice and how it relates to a traditional understanding of management. This section examines the customary laws[5] considered as Indigenous natural resource management in the region. Our focus was not based on comprehending the Bangladeshi government's meanings of management so much as seeking to understand Indigenous meanings of "management" and its significance in Indigenous people's everyday lives. Throughout the research, participants communicated that the community's understandings of management are interconnected with a number of common practices such as agriculture, traditional administration, traditional economics, and spirituality.

AGRICULTURE AND MANAGEMENT

Agriculture has been explained as vital to understanding the meaning of environmental management practices. The community's traditional agricultural domain was conceptualized by participants as a web of interrelated and multidirectional relationships during the first and second traditional sharing circle discussions. Several significant aspects of the agriculture domain were discussed by study participants, including crop varieties, forest resources, cultivation tools, and domestic animals.

TYPES OF CROPS

Particular crops play a major role in land and water management practices within the community. Elders and knowledge holders have confirmed that particular crops were regarded as highly as family members, and therefore had a monumental impact on the actions of other family members. These effects—such as a farmer's decision-making processes, cultivation methods, financial savings, and spiritual celebrations—were of crucial importance. There are three kinds of paddy crops produced in the Khyeng community, as explained by Elders: binni crop, which is most commonly used in spiritual practices and special occasions; jhum crop,[6] used for everyday use; and plain land crops or common paddy crops, similar to the jhum crop. To explain land, water, and forest management, participants discussed the meanings of these three different types of paddy crops and the influence they have on everyday management practices. The participants emphasized that the various crops offer and require different forms of management. For example, the Khyeng community's inspiration for cultivation is a symbol of forest diversity and protection and a sign of culture and financial solvency.

FOREST RESOURCES

The forest resources represent an important source of community's land, water, and environment management. Elders and knowledge holders consider forest resources as forested land and hilly land—in other words, jhum land embodied with wild animals, birds, and water sources. These forest resources provide many gifts. Elders have explained this as an opportunity for everyday management practices in the community. For example, these gifts include the space to grow edible vegetables and paddy crops, animals for hunting, bamboo for housing, and plants for medicine and spirituality. Such forms of management practices create equal accessibility in the community. For instance, the community members have equal rights to the hilly land and water sources. Moreover, this access enables the community to practice their ancestors' spirituality.

CULTIVATION TOOLS

The environmental resource management practices largely depend on the community's traditional cultivation tools, including the sword, the spear, and the knife. These three kinds of cultivation tools have many different functions in the community's management practices. Elders and knowledge holders discussed how the sword and the spear symbolized power of judgment for land distribution within the community. Sword and spear holders are considered respected and knowledgeable individuals. The number of swords and spears are symbolic of the economic strength of the community and related to a food surplus, and therefore a symbol of protection power. Knives represent fertility and hard work. The Khyeng men and woman all have equal access to these tools, and all are welcome to participate in cultivating the fields for the purpose of producing food, whereas other non-Indigenous Bangladeshi people have contrasting methods of practice (Adnan 2004). For example, one of our co-researcher participants demonstrated in their commonplace book that the Khyeng women produced their food with their cultivation tools and sold or exchanged their produce in their village market. The Khyeng women are able to hold these tools and play major decision-making roles within their own families as well as their communities.

DOMESTIC ANIMALS

Domestic animals represent a significant domain for the community's land, water, and forest management. The correlation between domestic animals and traditional management practices is described in the data as bestowing different degrees of social and economic prestige within the community. Having a domestic animal means more economic security, a more esteemed reputation, and added prestige for the entire family. However, because domestic animals are considered protector gods for the Khyeng, the conversion of domestic animals into monetary currency does not have equal meaning in terms of prestige and social reputation in the community. During the research gathering, Elders clarified that different domestic animals have varied influences on a community's sense of management practices. The Khyeng do not traditionally sell their domestic animals for monetary gain, although those traditions have changed recently. For example, cattle, chickens, and goats have cash value in the local market. That value can be transformed into economic capital to obtain an education or daily goods, as well as labor for cultivation practices and other resource management. Additionally, Elders stated that although Khyeng domestic animal practices have recently changed, the community continues to be spiritually connected with their domestic animals in everyday life.

As researchers, we have learned that the agricultural domains have spiritual, relational, and economic values within the community and are able to be transformed into symbols of power, inspiration, and support for the community's everyday management practices.

TRADITIONAL ADMINISTRATIVE STRUCTURE AND MANAGEMENT

While the researchers were learning of the community's environmental management through data on agriculture domains, descriptions of traditional administrative structures were also discussed as being vital for the community's land, water, and forest practices. Elders and leaders have highlighted the Laitu Khyang geographic location as being an important phenomenon for exploring relationships between the community's modes of administrative structure and understanding of management practices. For example, the Chittagong Hill Tracts are covered by three circles: the Bhonong circle, the Chakma circle, and the Mong circle.[7] The community's villages are mostly situated within the Bhomong circle (Adnan 2004). The traditional administrative structure involves three components: the village, the mouza (i.e., several villages), and the circle (i.e., several mouzas). Within each component, administrative positions are designated (Roy 2000). The first administrative position is the village manager, known as the Karbary; the second administrative position is known as the Headmen; and the third administrative position is known as the raja/king of the circle. Each administrative structure has different roles in management, but the three are all interconnected. The Indigenous villages have three Karbary positions, and they work with other Indigenous communities' Headmen and Circle Chiefs in mouzas and circles. These traditional administrative structures control land, water, and forest resource management in addition to distribution within the community.

Traditionally, the Circle Chief holds a significant role in protecting Indigenous spiritual and relational land, water, and forest management practices (Adnan 2004; Roy 2000). The Elders explain in their data that the Circle Chief's responsibilities have been changed since the time of their ancestors, resulting from interactions with both colonial (i.e., British, 1757–1947) and postcolonial state governments (i.e., Pakistan, 1947–71; Bangladesh, 1971–). However, the Elders still view the Circle Chief position with greater esteem than does the mainstream state administration. Elders and knowledge holders emphasized that proper knowledge about Indigenous communities' spiritual ceremonies and everyday management practices were the principal requisite for all three traditional administrative positions.

SPIRITUALITY AND MANAGEMENT

Research participants were eager to illuminate why spirituality was an important factor for practicing land, water, and forest management. The researchers were told that the community's everyday management practices with water, land, and forest were interconnected and aligned with their daily spiritual practices. For example, knowledge holder Kasamong Prue Khyeng justified the relationship between spirituality and management as follows: "If there is no spirituality, there is no community. For us spirituality represents taking care of our life and our environment." He explicitly describes the connectivity between spirituality and management in the following poem (translated by the Methuei Chaing Khyeng):

Our spirituality is our motherland.

Our spirituality is our hills, sky, water, and our heart.

Our spirituality always creates our relationships and our knowledge.

Our spirituality created us all in one family.

Our spirituality guides about us how to maintain our relationships with
land and water.

TRADITIONAL ECONOMY AND MANAGEMENT

The community's traditional economic community was discussed by participants as one of the significant factors in detailing the community's environmental management. During the second sharing circle conversation, Elders and knowledge holders made clear that, historically, the community observed a close relationship between management and daily economic activities, such as food production, food exchange, local market transactions, and food preservation. These relationships rely largely, but not entirely, on local input and skills from within the community. According to protocols of the traditional economy, decisions about purchasing various machines and minor equipment needed for economic activities are jointly made with other Indigenous and a small number of non-Indigenous communities.

Participants describe management in regard to the relational and ceremonial spiritual function of the domains outlined above. Illustrating the point, Elder Kosomo Prure Kheyng depicts relationships between agriculture domains and management practices as interconnected "everyday ceremonies."

Challenges of Current Management

This study illuminated the community's perceptions of the different agencies' land, water, and forest resource management projects within the community. In explaining the community's perceptions of current management practices, participants[8] often told us that rather than contributing to the community's security, the Bangladeshi governmental and nongovernment agencies' management projects engendered feelings of exploitation, frustration, fear, and danger, posing a formidable challenge to the community (see Figure 2).

EXPLOITATION

A sentiment of exploitation was frequently conveyed by participants when discussing governmental and nongovernment land and forest management projects in the community. For example, youth leader, activist, and co-researcher Hla Aung Prue Khyeng wrote in his commonplace book, "The current management projects became tools to grab our land." The various agencies' forest and plain land-management strategies are perceived by members

FIGURE 2. Profitable plantation project over natural forest. The top part of the photo depicts a profitable commercial plantation, and bottom part shows a natural forest. This picture is representative of many hills in the community.

of his community to be mechanisms of exploitation.[9] Similarly, knowledge-holder Kasamong Prue Khyeng linked non-Indigenous management projects to the struggles suffered within the community: "Today we are experiencing food crises and poverty as a result of our government imposing the exploit-ative land- and water-management projects on our traditional land, water, and forest. All of these current projects are nothing but exploitation to us." Most participants pointed out that since forced management projects have become commonplace in their community, exploitation has become increas-ingly evident.

FRUSTRATION

Leader, activist, and co-researcher Kray Prue Khyeng characterized the cur-rent management projects as "a root of frustration for us." Two predominant aspects fuelling the participants' frustration include outsiders' power over Indigenous community members and efforts to maximize profits from the community's forest. For example, knowledge holder Ching Sho Khyeng stated that the current management projects "are not only hopeless to us but are also seriously oppressive to our Mother Nature." The data revealed that frustration was a common response of community members reflecting on governmental and nongovernmental management projects.

FEAR

Current land and forest management projects enacted within the community elicit a profound fear that spiritual connections and relationships with trees, birds, animals, and plants are being damaged. Co-researcher participant Mathui Ching Khyang depicted the various agencies' management projects as "evil snakes to us" (a symbol of fear within the community). She described the government and development agencies' projects that way because the "management projects have been intentionally abusing our Mother Nature and displacing us." Elder Kosomo Prue Khyeng reiterated Mathui Ching Khyang's characterization that such projects are a source of fear within the community, stating, "We pass our days with serious fear for nightmare projects on our ancestors' land." Participants stressed that this fear continues to grow as the challenge to maintain the community's traditional management practices becomes increasingly difficult.

DANGER

Current management projects are also explained by participants in regard to representing a danger to the community. Community Elders and knowledge holders have explored reasons the government land management projects are seen as a danger to the community. One Elder emphasized that the different agencies and their management projects are designed "to cut and clear our forest by the name of the unproductive land. These projects are dangerous as they are grabbing our motherland to displace us." Participants detailed in the data-gathering process how the community's forestland and water bodies were transformed into sources of profit for the different agencies' projects. For instance, the knowledge holders emphasized that most of the projects have created serious challenges for the community's traditional management practices. Co-researcher participant Mathui Khyeng questioned outsider profit-making processes as follows: "Who is deciding our practices and management projects for us? Why do they not count our knowledge on our development projects? Who is responsible for creating poverty in our community? We know our government knew this, but they would not solve this. Our government wants to keep us unprotected through their artificial management projects." Participants emphasized that management and profit making were synonymous for outsider management organizations.

It is clear from the contributions of the participants that the various agencies' conceptions of management diverge from the community's understandings and practices. Taken together, the detrimental effects of current management projects (exploitation, frustration, fear, and danger) challenge the legitimacy of the projects and the organizations that administer them. Participants discussed their objections regarding settler occupation in which land grabbing, profit making, and displacement are achieved. Elder Basa Khyeng argued that the different agencies' anti-community management projects have rendered the community essentially unsustainable. Together with Elder Basa Khyeng, additional Elders and leaders outlined how various agencies' management projects contributed to the instability of the community through diminishing the community's ability to provide for itself and lead full lives.

Discussion

This study has acknowledged the importance of the community's traditional understandings and management practices (Battiste 2000; Tuck and McKenzie 2015). The study's findings revealed that participants value knowledge of Indigenous everyday practices when it comes to explanations of the community's perceptions of management. As we discussed, the Indigenous meanings of management have different meanings from the Western understandings of management (Berkes 2009, 2004; Nadasdy 2003). This difference may be illuminated along the following lines: the Western sense of environmental management has been widely criticized as positioning humans (particularly Western men) as a superior life form with an inherent right to use and control nature toward individualistic ends (Escobar 2008). Indigenous worldviews, in contrast, have been broadly defined, in various ways, as "a cumulative body of knowledge, practice and belief, evolving by adaptive processes, and handed down through generations by cultural transmission, about the relationship of living beings (including humans) with one another and their environment" (Berkes 2009, 7). In our study, researchers and participants identified the Laitu Khyeng community's concept of management knowledge from the cumulative body of knowledge as practice-based, holistic, spiritual, and relational.

PRACTICE-BASED
To the Laitu Khyeng Indigenous community, management practice honors the diversity of everyday life, which includes modes of agricultural spheres (i.e., domestic animals, cultivation tools, types of paddy crops, and forest resources). Such diverse aspects of management represent various agencies in their management practices, each having its own management power in

everyday practice. According to the participants, each component has an influence on the community's production, consumption, needs, time, surplus, and distribution. Elder Kosomo Prue Khyeng expressed in the data that "each animal, plant, and species has its own management power." He also clarified that community members do not believe management is a power that can be used over another; rather, they believe that management comprises different types of living relationships that have the ability to influence management practices. Similar studies (e.g., Berkes 1999; Simpson 2010) have argued that ideas of management practiced within Indigenous communities have diverse meanings and agency.

HOLISTIC

A second management dimension foundational to the Laitu Khyeng Indigenous community involves holistic sharing power through traditional administrative processes. As an example of this power-sharing practice, the community makes resource management decisions through participatory dialogue among community members. Berkes (2009) discusses power sharing in Indigenous management as a complex process (see also Nadasdy 2003). Power sharing can be seen as a move toward equity, as in the case of land distribution processes among Indigenous communities in Canada, Australia, Norway, and elsewhere. In the study, we observed that management is enacted through power sharing that has been overseen by traditional administrative structures. In this traditional administrative process, everybody owns rights concerning production and distribution. This aligns with the suggestion of Borrini-Feyerbend, Kothari, and Oviedo (2004, 175) that "participatory traditional management needs participatory roots."

DIVERSITY

Traditional management is discussed in the data as a process of building knowledge diversity among the community. The sharing of traditional knowledge and stories by Elders and knowledge-holders (regarding planting, cultivating, fishing, clothing, and spiritual celebrations) is considered a diverse social-capital building process within the community. We co-researcher participants noted that the youth who participated in evening story-sharing circles with their Elders experienced trust-building and acquired diverse knowledge. They learned how to recognize the purpose and behaviors of plants and animals, how to build relationships, and how to care for these plants and animals. Nadasdy (2003) considers diversity in natural resource management a form of social capital. It appears to be a determinant of success across generations in a diversity of management processes: a requisite to building and sharing knowledge as well as fostering effective relationships (Berkes 2009).

For example, Elder Basa Khyeng stated, "Our land, water, forest, and animals are our parents. They take care us, and our responsibilities are to take care them. Therefore, we cannot sell them or use them for profit." In addition to a sentiment of responsibility, participants emphasized that the community's management practices have multiple benefits: nothing can be owned as an individual commodity, and everything belongs to everyone; they build relational trust; and they construct supportive, respectful, and honorable attitudes among community members. The trust-building processes in environmental resources management allows us to recognize others as ourselves (Escobar 2008; Latour 2004; Li 2002). In such trust-building arrangements, everything is considered to belong to the community (Adnan 2004; Escobar 2008). As Martusewicz (2009, 258) suggested, common practices are helpful "at protecting larger life systems that we need and thus we are actively engaging and protecting collaborative intelligence."

SPIRITUAL AND RELATIONAL

The Laitu Khyeng Indigenous communities view their spiritual and relational management practices with the environment as having scientific and ecological significance. The researchers identified examples from the discussion of participants, photovoice, and commonplace books in which Laitu Khyeng Indigenous management practices offered solutions to multiple ecological and sociological issues. We discovered that traditional spiritual and relational management can reduce species extraction, water crises, logging, weeds, and food crises; and that traditional management knowledge increases diversity in plant and animal species, decision-making power among woman, youth empowerment, production of organic fertilizers, crop selection, and surplus distribution. Participants also expressed that common and scientific meanings of management practices are essential for reconstructing the Laitu Khyeng Indigenous identity, culture, and sustainable livelihood. Such a narrative can offer the opportunity to reconstruct, communicate, and reclaim Laitu Khyeng Indigenous traditional practices of natural resource management. As Berkes (1999) discussed on a similar note, Indigenous traditional management practices are scientific knowledge. Berkes explained that Indigenous traditional knowledge promotes the protection of remaining components of biodiversity and the unique values of local cultures; in addition, it can enhance the ability of local communities to establish a livelihood.

In other words, Indigenous traditional management practices and understandings are considered successful for natural resource management with respect to social, political, economic, and ecological domains (Reo 2011). Bohensky and Maru (2011) also suggest that in seeking practical solutions to environmental and socioeconomic impacts, local Indigenous management knowledge is a vital resource. Visions of community's management can be seen as relational and scientific practices in opposition to the West. In addition, Indigenous and non-Indigenous scholars (Lertzman 2010; Nadasdy 1999; Escobar 2010) explain that Indigenous people now engage with many decentralized approaches to environmental management, which offer opportunities for integration of Indigenous environmental management and Western science to promote cultural diversity within the management of social—ecological system sustainability.

Recommendations

To analyze community practice-based management, this article began by casting a critical eye at the notion of management. Elders, knowledge holders, leaders, and youth, through community-oriented management, call for a sincere attempt to recognize traditional knowledge that will promote and protect its values and encourage sustainability. The Elders, knowledge holders, leaders, and youth suggested a number of recommendations for bridging gaps between current state management policies and community, practice-oriented management. Community participants are committed to learning both Indigenous and non-Indigenous cultivation knowledge and practices. We advocate the application of the Indigenous, traditional, practice-based environmental resource management by policy makers and researchers. We look forward to future evaluations of its general effectiveness in guiding practitioners and researchers of scientific and Indigenous knowledge integration in environmental management. We would like to see the traditional cultivation culture and practices be recognized as equivalent to the state management system. How to successfully use both Indigenous and Western meanings of management is a task that differs between approaches. Our Indigenous Elders and knowledge holders suggested the following recommendations for the protection of traditional cultivation, cultures, and ways of life:

- Governmental and nongovernment environmental resource management policies and practices that ensure protection for traditional cultivation and culture must be adopted.
- Management policies and alliances must be formed with the Laitu Khyeng Indigenous peoples to defend their plain lands, forest lands, and water lands from exploitative development and to advocate for the resolution of outstanding issues. There is a need to recognize Indigenous administrative structure, where the resolution of these issues will strengthen the capacity of Laitu Khyeng people to protect their environmental resources and promote their sustainability.
- Indigenous people must be supported to defend themselves from unwanted developmental management threats, including reserve forests, tobacco plantations, brickfield industrial companies, and lumber plantations.

- Governmental and multinational environmental agencies must recognize the value of traditional knowledge and practices in Indigenous environmental resource protection and develop working relationships with Indigenous people based on their value and culture.

These recommendations are vital parameters to improving the environment and to protecting Indigenous people's identity and culture. Policies and programs to address Indigenous sustainability, in particular those environmental management issues that have an important role in Indigenous culture, need to be Indigenous-led, where Indigenous peoples are the key decision makers on issues that affect their lands and, therefore, their livelihoods and well-being.

RANJAN KUMAR DATTA is an independent researcher and research facilitator in the College of Education at the University of Saskatchewan.

JEBUNNESSA CHAPOLA is a Ph.D. candidate in the Department of Woman's, Gender, and Sexuality Studies at the University of Saskatchewan.

Notes

We are grateful to the Laitu Khyeng Indigenous Elders, knowledge holders, leaders, and youth participants who so warmly welcomed us to their community and provided opportunities to learn their land—water management and sustainability stories. We are also enormously grateful to our four co-researcher participants—Nyojy U. Khyang, Hla Kray Prue Khyang, Hla Aung Prue Kheyang, and Mathui Ching Khyang—for joining in this research team and for their continuous support. We also want to thank Dr. Ranjan Datta's Ph.D. adviser Dr. Marcia McKenzie and committee member Dr. Alex Wilson. Both of you have been motivating, encouraging, and enlightening mentors.

1. The term *we* refers to a collective research team and collective ways of conducting research as part of participatory action research (PAR) (Datta 2015). The term "we" includes university researchers, community participants, Elders, knowledge holders, leaders, and four co-researcher participants. *We*, as a collective research team, were continuously engaged and participated through field research and data analysis processes, such as identifying research questions; facilitating traditional sharing circles; conducting participant observation and photovoice; recording traditional sharing circles and individual storytelling discussions; maintaining a commonplace book, which we used to record personal observations, art, poems, experiences, stories with the environment, and field notes; and helping to code and analyze research data (Datta et al. 2014). *In this research, youth and co-researcher participants were requested to take pictures of their home—focusing on plants, animals, birds, land, the moon, rocks, and so on—and then shared their stories connected to their particular pictures, which we named photovoice.* Researcher and co-researcher participants conducted

research according to the guidelines and suggestions of the community's Elders, knowledge holders, and leaders.

2. Laitu Khyeng Indigenous people comprise those who are inhabitants of Gungru Muke Para and Gungru Madom Para (village) in the Bandarban district CHT Bangladesh (Adnan 2004; Chapola 2008).

3. The term "extinction" refers here to the CHT Indigenous traditional way of life. See Adnan 2004 for more information.

4. The plain land population in CHT is referred as a mainstream non-Indigenous people of Bangladesh (Adnan 2004).

5. According to the Elder Basa Khyeng, the customary laws are the ancestral ways of life that their community and other Indigenous communities have been practicing for generations.

6. Different kinds of paddy crops, vegetables, fruit, and other cash crops.

7. "Circle" here is utilized to represent the CHT Indigenous communities' geographical designation. A circle corresponds to a district (Adnan 2004). The term is used here for explaining the Laitu Khyeng Indigenous' traditional administrative structure in relation to their natural resource management practices.

8. In some parts of this section we have included participants' information, and in some parts we have not disclosed participants' information in accordance with their preferences.

9. The plain cultivated area is mostly situated beside hilly areas (Adnan 2004).

Bibliography

Adnan, S. 2004. *Migration Land Alienation and Ethnic Conflict: Causes of Poverty in the Chittagong Hill Tracts of Bangladesh*. Dhaka, Bangladesh: Research and Advisory Services.

Adnan, S., and R. Dastidar. 2011. *Mechanisms of Land Alienation of the Indigenous Peoples of the Chittagong Hill Tracts: Report of Study Undertaken for the Chittagong Hill Tracts Commission*. Copenhagen: IWGIA.

Aikenhead, G. S., & M. Ogawa. 2007. "Indigenous Knowledge and Science Revisited." *Cultural Studies of Science Education* 2: 539–620.

Battiste, M. 2000. "Maintaining Aboriginal Identity, Language, and Culture in Modern Society." In *Reclaiming Indigenous Voice and Vision*, edited by M. Battiste, 192–208. Toronto: University of British Columbia Press.

Battiste, M., and J. Y. Henderson. 2000. *Protecting Indigenous Knowledge and Heritage: A Global Challenge*. Saskatoon, Canada: Purich.

Berkes, F. 1999. *Sacred Ecology: Traditional Ecological Knowledge and Resource Management*. Philadelphia: Taylor and Francis.

———. 2004. "Rethinking Community-Based Conservation." *Conservation Biology* 18, no. 3: 621–30.

———. 2009. "Evolution of Co-management: Role of Knowledge Generation, Bridging Organizations, and Social Learning." *Journal of Environmental Management* 90: 1692–1702.

Bohensky, E. L., and Y. Maru. 2011. "Indigenous Knowledge, Science, and Resilience: What Have We Learned from a Decade of International Literature on 'Integration'?" *Ecology and Society* 16, no. 4: 6.

Borrini-Feyerabend, A. G. Kothari, and G. Oviedo. 2004. *Indigenous and Local Communities and Protected Areas*. Cambridge, U.K.: IUCN.

Briggs, J. 2005. "The Use of Indigenous Knowledge in Development: Problems and Challenges." *Progress in Development Studies* 5, no. 2: 99–114.

Briggs, J., and J. Sharp. 2004. "Indigenous Knowledges and Development: A Postcolonial Caution." *Third World Quarterly* 25, no. 4: 661–76.

Brosius, P. 1997. "Endangered Forests, Endangered People: Environmentalist Representations of Indigenous Knowledge." *Human Ecology* 25, no. 1: 47–69.

Butler, J. R. A., A. Tawake, T. Skewes, L. Tawake, and V. McGrath. 2012. "Integrating Traditional Ecological Knowledge and Fisheries Management in the Torres Strait, Australia: The Catalytic Role of Turtles and Dugong as Cultural Keystone Species." *Ecology and Society* 17, no. 4: 34.

Chapin, F. S., III, S. R. Carpenter, G. P. Kofinas, C. Folke, N. Abel, W. C. Clark, P. Olsson, D. M. S. Smith, B. Walker, O. R. Young, F. Berkes, R. Biggs, J. M. Grove, R. L. Naylor, E. Pinkerton, W. Steffen, and F. J. Swanson. 2010. "Ecosystem Stewardship: Sustainability Strategies for a Rapidly Changing Planet." *Trends in Ecology and Evolution* 25: 241–49.

Chapola, J. 2008. *Labour Migration, Inter-ethnic Relations, and Empowerment: A Study of Khyang Indigenous Garments Workers, Chittagong Hill Tracts, Bangladesh*. Bergen, Norway: University of Bergen.

Gupta, A. Das. 2009. "The Relevance of 'Indigenous Peoples': A Case Study of the Rajbansi Community of North Bengal." In *Environment and Sustainable Development in India*, edited by A. Mukherjee with P. K. Pal and R. K. Sen, 11–129. New Delhi: Deep and Deep.

———. 2011. "Does Indigenous Knowledge Have Anything to Deal with Sustainable Development?" *Antrocom Online Journal of Anthropology* 7, no. 1: 57–64.

Datta, R. 2015. "A Relational Theoretical Framework and Meanings of Land, Nature, and Sustainability for Research with Indigenous Communities." *International Journal of Justice and Sustainability* 20, no. 1: 102–13.

Datta, R., N. Khyeng, H. Khyeng, M. Khyeng, and J. Chapola, J. 2014. "Participatory Action Research and Researcher's Responsibilities: An Experience with Indigenous Community." *International Journal of Social Research Methodology* 18, no. 6.

Dudgeon, R. C., and F. Berkes. 2003). "Local Understandings of the Land: Traditional Ecological Knowledge And Indigenous Knowledge." In *Nature across Cultures*, edited by H. Selin, 75–96. Dordrecht: Kluwer Academic.

Escobar, A. 1995. "Power and Visibility: Tales of Peasants, Women, and Environment." In *Encountering Development: The Making and Unmaking of the Third World*, edited by A. Escobar, 154–211. Princeton, N.J.: Princeton University Press.

———. 2008. *Territories of Difference: Place, Movements, Life, Redes*. Durham, N.C.: Duke University Press.

————. 2010. "Latin America at a Crossroads." *Cultural Studies* 24, no. 1: 1—65.

Fletcher, R. 2009. "Ecotourism Discourse: Challenging the Stakeholders Theory." *Journal of Ecotourism* 8, no. 3: 269—85.

Folke, C. 2004. "Traditional Knowledge in Social—Ecological Systems." *Ecology and Society* 9, no. 3: 7.

Gadgil, M., F. Berkes, and C. Folke. 1993. "Indigenous Knowledge for Biodiversity Conservation." *Ambio* 22: 151—56.

Harvey, D. 2005. *A Brief History of Neoliberalism*. Oxford, U.K.: Oxford University Press.

Latour, B. 2004. *Polities of Management: How to Bring the Sciences into Democracy*. Translated by Catherine Porter. Cambridge, Mass.: Harvard University Press.

Lertzman, D. A. 2010. "Best of Two Worlds: Traditional Ecological Knowledge and Western Science in Ecosystem-Based Management." *BC Journal of Ecosystems and Management* 10, no. 3: 104—26.

Lertzman, D. A., and H. Vredenburg, H. 2005. "Indigenous Peoples, Resource Extraction, and Sustainable Development: An Ethical Approach." *Journal of Business Ethics* 56: 239—54.

Lévi-Strauss, C. 1968. *The Savage Mind: The Management of Human Society*. Chicago: University of Chicago Press.

Li, T. 2002. "Engaging Simplifications: Community-Based Natural Resource Management, Market Processes, and State Agendas in Upland Southeast Asia." *World Development* 30, no. 2: 265—83.

Little Bear, L. 2009. *Naturalizing Indigenous Knowledge: Synthesis Paper*. Saskatoon: University of Saskatchewan Aboriginal Education Research Centre and First Nations and Adult Higher Education Consortium.

Martusewicz, R. 2009. "Educating for 'Collaborative Intelligence': Revitalizing the Cultural and Ecological Commons in Detroit." In *Fields of Green: Restorying, Culture, Environment, and Education*, edited by M. McKenzie, P. Hart, H. Bai, and B. Jickling, 253—67. Cresskill, N.J.: Hampton.

Mohsin, A. 1997. *The Politics of Nationalism: The Case of the Chittagong Hill Tracts*. Dhaka, Bangladesh: University Press.

2002. *The Polities of Nationalism: The Case of the Chittagong Hill Tracts, Bangladesh*. Dhaka, Bangladesh: University Press.

Nadasdy, P. 1999. The Politics of TEK: Power and the 'Integration" of Knowledge." *Arctic Anthropology* 36, nos. 1—2: 1—18.

————. 2003. "Reevaluating the Co-management Success Story." *Arctic* 5: 367—80.

————. 2011. "We Don't Harvest Animals; We Kill Them: Agricultural Metaphors and the Politics of Wildlife Management in the Yukon." In *Knowing Management*, edited by M. Goldman, P. Nadasdy, & M. D. Turner, 135—51. Chicago: University of Chicago Press.

Nakanura, N. 2008. "An 'Effective' Involvement of Indigenous People in Environmental Impact Assessment: The Cultural Impact Assessment of the Saru River Region, Japan." *Australian Geographer* 39: 427—44.

Reo, N. J. 2011. "The Importance of Belief Systems in Traditional Ecological Knowledge Initiatives." *International Indigenous Policy Journal* 2, no. 4: 1—3.

Roy, C. R. 2000. *Land Rights of the Indigenous Peoples of the Chittagong Hill Tracts, Bangladesh.* Copenhagen: IWGIA.

Schendel, V. W., W. Mey, and K. A. Dewan. 2001. *The Chittagong Hill Tracts: Living in a borderland.* Dhaka, Bangladesh: University Press.

Simpson, L. 2004. "Anticolonial Strategies for the Recovery and Maintenance of Indigenous Knowledge." *American Indian Quarterly* 28 (2004): 373–84.

Spivak, G. C. 2006. "Can the Subaltern Speak?" In *The Neo-Colonial Studies Reader*, edited by B. Ashcroft, G. Griffiths, and H. Tiffin, 28–37. New York: Routledge.

Sumara, D. J. 1996. "Using Commonplace Books in Curriculum Studies." *Journal of Curriculum Theorizing* 12: 45–48.

Thapa, G. B., & G. Rasul. 2006. "Implications of Changing National Policies on Land Use in the Chittagong Hill Tracts of Bangladesh." *Journal of Environmental Management* 81: 441–53.

Tuck, E., and M. McKenzie. 2015. *Place in Research: Theory, Methodology, Methods.* New York: Routledge.

United Nations Development Programme. 2013. "The Knowledge Of Indigenous Peoples and Policies for Sustainable Development: Updates and Trends in the Second Decade of the World's Indigenous People." http://www.un.org/.

Walker, B. H., and D. Salt. 2006. *Resilience Thinking: Sustaining Ecosystems and People in a Changing World.* Washington, D.C.: Island Press.

Wilson, S. 2008. *Research Is Ceremony: Indigenous Research Methods.* Winnipeg: Fernwood.

Wright, L., and J. White, J. 2012. "Developing Oil and Gas Resources on or Near Indigenous Lands in Canada: An Overview of Laws, Treaties, Regulations, and Agreements." *International Indigenous Policy Journal* 3, no. 2.

Xu, J., E. T. Ma, D. Tashi, Y. Fu, Z. Lu, and D. Melick. 2006. "Integrating Sacred Knowledge for Conservation: Cultures and Landscapes in Southwest China." *Ecology and Society* 10, no. 2: 7.

Young, R. 2003. *Postcolonialism: A Very Short Introduction.* New York: Oxford University Press.

JONATHAN CLAPPERTON

Apostate Englishman: Grey Owl the Writer and the Myths
by Albert Braz
University of Manitoba Press, 2015

WHILE NUMEROUS non-Indigenous people cast in movies—including Espera Oscar de Corti (Iron Eyes Cody)—along with scholars and writers such as Ward Churchill and Joseph Boyden, have faced serious backlash for lying about, misrepresenting, or not being entirely clear about their self-identification as Indigenous, arguably the most well-known and controversial is Grey Owl / Archibald Belaney. Born in England, Belaney subsequently moved to Canada where he would adopt the name "Grey Owl" and assume an Indigenous identity, gaining fame through his many publications and lectures that advocated for environmental conservation.

Albert Braz's *Apostate Englishman: Grey Owl the Writer and the Myths* explores what Grey Owl "had actually written and the relation between those writings and the ever-increasing representations of him" (xiv). *Apostate Englishman* thus consists of two aspects: how Grey Owl / Archibald Belaney saw himself as expressed through his writing, and how others—his family, friends, publishers, critics, and supporters—described him. Through such analysis, Braz convincingly demonstrates that Grey Owl's advocacy for wildlife became inseparable from his apparent Indigeneity.

After a brief discussion of Archibald Belaney's early biography, Braz provides, in chapters 2 and 3, a close reading of *Pilgrims of the Wild*, *Sajo and the Beaver People*, *Tales of an Empty Cabin*, and other writings. Braz then, in chapter 4, examines the relationship between Anahareo and Grey Owl during and after their marriage through her published work and personal correspondence. Chapter 5 analyzes the controversial aftermath of Grey Owl's death in 1938, including histories, poems, letters, and other commentary, as well as the movie *Grey Owl* (1999).

What sets this book apart from many other studies of Grey Owl is that it goes far beyond an analysis of Grey Owl's published material. Braz has combed through piles of correspondence to better understand Grey Owl and how others saw him. Doing so illuminates personal connections among Grey Owl's reviewers, publishers, and others, and personalizes Grey Owl's writings beyond just his autobiography to reveal his personal struggles, fantasies, desires, regrets, worldview, and other aspects of his life and of those people who were close to him.

However, the least satisfying aspect of *Apostate Englishman* is Braz's handling of the issue of cultural appropriation. Since his death, Grey Owl has been viscerally denunciated—a "level of vitriol" Braz claims is perplexing. He argues that instead of condemning Belaney for appropriating another culture, what actually "troubled many people was not so much that Grey Owl had fooled them about his identity and embraced the North American Indigenous way of life but the fact that he had forsaken European culture. That is, he had committed cultural apostasy" (1). In some instances, Braz may be right in adding another layer to answer why Belaney and others like him elicit such harsh criticism. But this added nuance does not dismiss or counter criticisms of Belaney, as Braz attempts to do multiple times throughout the book, even asserting that some of those who criticize Grey Owl are unable to "understand [or] forgive" his cultural apostasy and so "accuse him of cultural appropriation" (172). Such critics are not "accusing" Grey Owl of anything; rather, they are stating what he consciously did. Indeed, Braz himself provides ample evidence of Belaney's deception.

Rather than focusing on Belaney's dishonesty, Braz would have us instead look to Grey Owl for literary and environmental inspiration. Given that Braz's argument centered on the inseparable connections between Grey Owl, Indigeneity, and the environment, it was extremely surprising to find no engagement with, or even citations of others who identify, the problems caused by the perpetuation of what has been termed the "ecological Indian" stereotype. Consequently, the greatest drawback in *Apostate Englishman* is its rather large blind spot to the violence that settler-colonial cultural appropriation and, to borrow from Philip Deloria, "playing Indian," does to Indigenous peoples.

JONATHAN CLAPPERTON is an assistant professor in the Department of History at the Memorial University of Newfoundland.

SUZI HUTCHINGS

The Politics of Identity: Who Counts as Aboriginal Today?
by Bronwyn Carlson
Aboriginal Studies Press, 2016

THE POLITICS OF IDENTITY: WHO COUNTS AS ABORIGINAL TODAY? is a timely study by Bronwyn Carlson on the historical construction of Aboriginal identities in Australia. Carlson's book comes on the heels of increasing debate in Australia among Indigenous and non-Indigenous academics, social commentators, politicians, journalists, and Aboriginal people alike on what can be classed as legitimate criteria for a person to claim an Aboriginal identity. In 2001 Mick Gooda, Australia's Aboriginal and Torres Strait Islander social justice commissioner at the time, stated, "Surely it is vital that every individual has the power to shape their own identity—to stand up and say 'this is who I am and this is what I believe' without that certainty being challenged? For Australia's Aboriginal and Torres Strait Islander population, however, this has rarely been the case" ("One's Identity Is for the Individual to Interpret," *Sydney Morning Herald*, November 24, 2001). Since then, public debate has increased in intensity, with senior Aboriginal leaders and academics joining the discussion. Carlson's book is an important contribution to this conversation.

In a compelling introduction, Carlson interweaves her family history and her developing understanding of the composition of her own Aboriginality with a commentary on the emerging politics of identity in Australia over the past forty years. Carlson juxtaposes this analysis with an exposé of officially accepted definitions of the criteria used to confirm Aboriginal identity. In this discussion, Carlson skillfully exposes the contradictions between personal, Aboriginal community, and government definitions of what characteristics delineate an Aboriginal person.

Carlson's book is based on the extensive research she undertook as part of her doctoral thesis. Most important, her study is conducted from within an Aboriginal perspective where her own Aboriginality has been rigorously scrutinized over time by herself, her family, her peers, and the wider Indigenous and non-Indigenous community in which she now lives and works. Carlson's personal journey has compelled her to critically review the extensive research already undertaken in Australia on the history of state and federal policies and legislation and the church and welfare interventions under which Aboriginal people in Australia have been forced to live. She concentrates her review particularly on the period since the 1900s, which continues to have profound resonances for how Aboriginal people from all walks of life see themselves in contemporary Australian society.

Carlson's book is presented in two parts. Part 1 "begins by looking at the colonial construction of Aboriginality" (15) and then ventures into an exploration of the period from the 1960s until 1988. She then explores the literature of the 1970s to the present, looking at the shifts in focus on the "changing meanings of Aboriginal identity" (15). In part 1 Carlson relies heavily on the primary research, analysis, and quotes of historical and anthropological materials developed by others such as McCorquodale, Reynolds, and Langton in the formulation of her own ideas on the issue of Aboriginal identity as constructed socially and historically in Australia.

In part 2 Carlson "deals with the contemporary contests of Aboriginality" and the confirmation of Aboriginality processes (15). In this section Carlson comes into her own with insightful evaluations of the political implications on the myriad people who claim Aboriginality within a contested identity space in contemporary Australian society. This group includes members of the Stolen Generation. Carlson's final chapter—"Concluding Remarks"—draws directly from the interviews used in her doctoral thesis. Carlson highlights the difficulties many Aboriginal people face in claiming an Aboriginal identity that is considered legitimate across politically diverse and often opposing platforms. These include Aboriginal communities, media commentary, universities, and the sphere of politics and government.

In concluding her book, Carlson admits she does not intend to resolve any of the issues she has raised about the contested identity space that is Aboriginality. Rather, her book is a call for further review and reflection, and in particular self-reflection by Aboriginal people, on "our own practices" and a compliance with government and other "official" regimes in determining definitions, reminiscences, and lived experiences of being Aboriginal in contemporary Australian society (273). Poignantly, she highlights the possibilities we can achieve, in "our relations with the wider nation-state" (273) if we are less preoccupied with the regulation and surveillance of our fellow Aboriginal Australians as to whether we are Aboriginal. Implicit in Carlson's stance on this is the fact that it remains a legacy of Indigenous relations with the "master" colonizer that we accept the crumbs he throws under the table for Indigenous society to collect, and it is the acceptance of this position that Aboriginal people must change in order to achieve (273).

SUZI HUTCHINGS (Arrernte, Central Australia) is a senior lecturer in the Indigenous Studies Unit, School of Global, Urban, and Social Studies, RMIT University.

KARL JACOBY

American Indians and National Forests
by Theodore Catton
University of Arizona Press, 2016

AMERICAN INDIANS may be popularly celebrated as the "first conservationists," but in reality the relationship between Native nations and conservationists has been vexed. The creation of national parks and national forests almost always involved Native dispossession, as the indigenous inhabitants of conservation areas were displaced by new administrators who saw Indian hunting, gathering, fishing, and fire-setting as nuisances at best and as crimes at worst. As a result, conservation became an integral part of settler colonialism. Not only did it function as one of the primary factors depriving Natives of access to natural resources; but by creating empty, unpopulated "wilderness" landscapes out of what had once been Indian homelands, conservation reinforced an ideology of erasure that obscured the Native presence in North America.

The place of national parks in this story has been ably recounted by historians such as Mark Spence (*Dispossessing the Wilderness*) and Louis Warren (*The Hunter's Game*). Theodore Catton extends this analysis to national forests in this important and useful new study. *American Indians and National Forests* began life as an administrative history, designed to record the experiences of the United States Forest Service's tribal relations program while many of the individuals involved in the process were still available for interviews. One of the virtues of Catton's approach, however, is that he does not limit his focus to just recent events, but rather traces the entire arc of interactions between federal forestry officials and Indian peoples. Readers are afforded concise overviews of such subjects as the efforts by Teddy Roosevelt and Gifford Pinchot to expand the national forest system, the Civilian Conservation Corps, and the termination policy, each paired with a case study that casts in sharp relief the pressures these developments placed on Natives. Many early forest reserves, for example, were carved out of Indian reservations, leading Native communities to grapple with the forests' new federal managers, be it through surreptitious resistance, informal arrangements such as the Yakama "handshake agreement" of 1932, or the lawsuit against the Tongass National Forest brought by the Tlingit and Haida in 1935.

This early history of conflict serves as a foil for later developments in *American Indians and National Forests*. Catton identifies the 1970s as a watershed moment in the relationship between Natives and the Forest Service. The Nixon administration's embrace of self-determination for tribal governments, coupled with the Forest Service's adoption of ecosystem management in place of maximum timber yield, created an opening for new arrangements to emerge. Establishing a workable system of nation-to-nation relations based on Native sovereignty, however, has not proven to be an easy task. Utilizing Forest Service records and oral histories, Catton guides readers through the bureaucratic infighting that led to the establishment of the Office of Tribal Relations in 2002 and its aftermath.

Part of the challenge was the diversity of ecosystems and American Indian communities with which the Forest Service interacted. While many tribes in the Pacific Northwest were signatories to treaties reserving them the right to fish at "usual and accustomed places" and to hunt and gather on "open and unclaimed lands," the majority of Native communities in California lacked treaties and/or a land base, requiring them to access public lands to practice their cultural traditions. While Native use of fire had been limited in the rainy Northwest, Indians in California had extensively manipulated their local ecosystems through proscribed burnings. Crafting a uniform policy that encompassed this wide range of conditions, without stressing the resources of tribal governments, already overburdened by "consultation fatigue" (278), remains an ongoing process for the Forest Service.

Some readers may question whether there has in fact been as much progress in the relationship between Native nations and the Forest Service as Catton portrays in *American Indians and National Forests*. It appears clear from Catton's evidence that the Forest Service over the past few decades has made a good-faith effort to involve once-excluded Native peoples in its decision-making process. But because his research is based primarily on Forest Service documents, the perspective of Native communities on recent events hovers in the background, brought out through occasional case studies (such as a very well-crafted chapter on the Nez Perce) but never occupying the foreground of his analysis.

KARL JACOBY is a professor in the History Department and the Center for the Study of Ethnicity and Race at Columbia University.

DREW CHRISTINA GONROWSKI

The World and All the Things upon It: Native Hawaiian Geographies
  of Exploration
by David Chang
Minneapolis: University of Minnesota Press, 2016

IN *THE WORLD AND ALL THE THINGS UPON IT: NATIVE HAWAIIAN GEOGRAPHIES OF EXPLORATION* historian David Chang examines the processes of global geography to counter histories that portray Kanaka Maoli and the Hawaiian Islands as passive subjects explored by Westerners. Chang's work confronts these colonial versions of history by focusing on the ways Kānaka Maoli explored, conceptualized, and defined their place in the world while highlighting Kanaka individuals, perspectives, and sources. Constructions of global geography, Chang argues, "became a site through which Hawaiians as well as their would-be colonizers understood and contested imperialism, colonialism, and nationalism" (vii). Throughout the book Chang traces how Kānaka constructed Kanaka global geographies and emphasizes that a "Hawaiian geography must be a *global* geography as well as a geography of the islands" (xiii). It is this global conceptualization of geography rooted in the Hawaiian Islands that guides the seven chapters in the book.

The first chapter centers the reader in the Hawaiian Islands by focusing on ways Kanaka understood the world in the eighteenth century. Analyzing sources such as mele (songs) and ʻōlelo noʻeau (proverbs and wise sayings), Chang begins his book by highlighting Kanaka forms of literature, history, and knowledge while discussing the history of Kanaka exploration and travel prior to the arrival of James Cook in 1778. The second chapter challenges European-centered histories of the Pacific and instead centers the perspective of early encounters in the Hawaiian Islands by emphasizing the ways Kānaka explored Europeans, European ships, and the world in the late 1700s. In the third chapter Chang discusses how Kānaka explored without leaving the Hawaiian Islands by using Christianity to obtain knowledge of the outside world. In doing so, Chang "reverses the geography and reverses the directionality of standard accounts of the advent of Christianity to Hawaiʻi" (80).

The fourth chapter traces the different geography textbooks used in Hawaiian classrooms in the 1800s to show how both "Kanaka educationalists" and "missionary and planter-aligned Haole educationalists" used schools and geography texts to educate Kānaka on their place in the world. Chang argues that "geography education was a site of contestation, but also a tool that Kānaka wielded in defense of their lāhui (nation)" (109). The fifth chapter explores connections between race and geography by examining the experiences of Kānaka living in California and New England and how they engaged with a system of race imposed by white Americans. By using Hawaiian-language newspapers and census records to focus on the experiences of individuals, Chang shows how Kānaka moved across spatial boundaries while simultaneously being limited by imposed racial characterizations as they lived in communities with American Indians in California and with black populations on Nantucket. Kanaka relationships with American Indians are revisited in chapter 7 as Chang traces several shifts in how Kānaka viewed themselves in comparison to American Indians, pointing to the effects of global processes, especially American colonialism.

Chapter 6 returns to the topic of Christianity and the geography of sacred power by discussing both Kanaka Christian missionary efforts to other Pacific Islands as well as wahi pana (storied places). Chang argues that moʻolelo (stories) and mele of wahi pana countered "missionary desacralization of the Hawaiian landscape" because they "asserted the mana of the sites of their archipelago against a colonialist geography that situated sacred power far away, in Western nations and biblical lands" (218, 224). In the book's epilogue Chang briefly discusses how Kānaka of the 1900s and 2000s are "part of the moʻokūʻauhau [genealogy] of exploration and of efforts by Kānaka to define their place in the world," showing that these efforts did not stop at the end of the 1800s (256).

Through examining the ways geography is interwoven in various topics such as race, labor, religion, and education, Chang takes a new approach to studying how Kānaka confronted the world in the 1800s. As Chang states, *The World and All the Things upon It* fits in with other studies of indigenous geographies that are "crucial to understanding the dispossession of indigenous people and working for ecological restoration and social justice" (xiii). By using global geography to show how Kānaka have been dispossessed and misrepresented in histories, Chang's work adds to the growing studies of indigenous geographies and to the fields of Hawaiian history and world history, challenging readers to rethink global encounters by centering such encounters on the perspectives and systems of knowledge of Kanaka Maoli.

DREW CHRISTINA GONROWSKI is a history instructor at the University of Hawaiʻi—West Oʻahu.

CAROLINE LEGAN

*Unconventional Politics: Nineteenth-Century Women Writers
and U.S. Indian Policy*
by Janet Dean
University of Massachusetts Press, 2016

IN HER NEW MONOGRAPH *Unconventional Politics: Nineteenth-Century Women Writers and U.S. Indian Policy*, Janet Dean interprets works about Native Americans by nineteenth-century female authors who used conventional genres of writing to protest against U.S. policies toward Native Americans. In doing so, she claims that these authors' unconventional politics transformed conventional literature.

Dean's work is organized into four chapters, and she focuses on several different authors, texts, and genres of writing in each one. She sees her subjects as not only politically driven but also political activists. For example, in chapter 3, Dean analyzes scenes of reading in two texts: Zitkala-Ša's "The School Days of an Indian Girl" and *Wynema: A Child of the Forest*. Dean argues that reading is a tool of oppression in the first text: propaganda used to indoctrinate former students of the Carlisle Indian Schools into white ways of thinking by ensuring they feel disconnected from and contempt for their Native communities. The second text encourages readers to read critically, question the narrative being presented, and undertake independent research. Thus, the first text is a critique of boarding school—era policies and the second encourages readers to think for themselves, both of which can be read as political activism.

Scholars have traditionally seen sentimental fiction about Native Americans as ripe with political undertones because it was a conventionally feminine print form that could tolerate political messages. In concentrating on print forms besides the sentimental novel, Dean exposes expressions of political resistance in the most unexpected places. She writes, "The genres my subjects adopted . . . typically helped sustain U.S. Indian policy. In most incarnations, these genres reinforced popular justifications for federal actions aimed at removing, managing or annihilating Native people. To repurpose these instruments for protest was to claim political *and* cultural agency" (6). In demonstrating the plasticity and political potency of her examined genres, Dean's work may inspire future scholars to reexamine genres that have traditionally been labeled nonpolitical.

Dean's work recalls Beth Piatote's 2013 monograph *Domestic Subjects: Gender, Citizenship, and Law in Native American Literature*. Piatote also writes about nineteenth-century female authors who protested U.S. policies toward and challenged dominant cultural stereotypes about Native Americans. Whereas Piatote focuses exclusively on sentimental fiction, Dean draws on different genres, thereby expanding on Piatote's claim that female authors who wrote about the "Indian problem" in the nineteenth century were advocating for social change in a manner that would have been conventionally appropriate for their sex at the time. Both Dean and Piatote must concede, however, that the authors they examine did more to expand the genres they worked in than to effect real social change for the Indians. Nevertheless, the voice of nineteenth-century female authors pushing back against dominant cultural tropes and critiquing U.S. Indian policy is an important protest to highlight, since it demonstrates that there were people at the time resisting the dominant narrative, exposing unpleasant truths, and imagining an alternative future that gave agency to Native Americans. Calling attention to the voices of those who spoke out on their behalf, especially in genres that were unconventionally political, demonstrates that disenfranchised people can and have voiced their political beliefs in the face of tradition and history.

Dean's work reminds us that, under careful scrutiny, seemingly apolitical conventional texts can actually be coded political protest. In completing this monograph, Dean has not only given voice to two groups that have been traditionally marginalized, but has also demonstrated how a person can become a simultaneous advocate for two social causes, advancing one through activism for the other. In that way, her work may inspire scholars to examine the secondary implications of various social protest movements, especially those beyond that movement's stated goal.

To examine four different genres of writing and demonstrate how their authors critiqued U.S. policies toward Indians is no easy feat. Dean has clearly thought about each of her points from multiple angles, and literary passages seem indefatigable for her analysis. Her ability to weave historical background information into her analysis of fiction lends credibility to her arguments. Dean's writing is focused, detailed, and unrelenting. It can be dense at times, so it is not a light read. But for anyone interested in nineteenth-century protest writing or feminist contributions to Native American studies, this book comes highly recommended.

CAROLINE LEGAN is a graduate student in the English Department at Louisiana State University.

SHANNON SPEARS

Pictures from My Memory: My Story as a Ngaatjatjarra Woman
by Lizzie Marrkilyi Ellis
Aboriginal Studies Press, 2016

PICTURES FROM MY MEMORY: MY STORY AS A NGAATJATJARRA WOMAN is a narrative-style text written by a proud Aboriginal woman, Elizabeth (Lizzie) Marrkilyi Ellis. However, her identity has been constructed through double consciousness, for she was raised not only in her Ngaatjatjarra community but also in a Western community. This is reflected in her book when she gives detailed life experiences from both her Ngaatjatjarra community and how it was affected by colonizers (or, as the author terms them, "whitefellas") and her Western lifestyle in Alice Springs.

Even though the author has lived a Western lifestyle, in which she attended Western schools and married a white man, she holds onto her traditions and customs from her Aboriginal community. One way her work reflects this is through the literary use of both the English language and her native language, Ngaatjatjarra. Another way is her work as a translator, connecting the Western world and the Aboriginal community. Additionally, the author explains how she still comes home to visit her family and participate in whatever traditions she can. Finally, she explains how she raised her daughters in a Western lifestyle but still teaches them Aboriginal customs by storytelling and visiting family members in the bush.

Lizzie Marrkilyi Ellis's book is a narrative-style text written in first person by an Aboriginal woman describing her life experiences as shaped through her double consciousness. Her writing is not biased when it comes to perspective. Her book is accessible, for she provides a glossary and thoroughly translates from Ngaatjatjarra to English.

The book begins with Lizzie Marrkilyi Ellis introducing herself and stating how she has always lived a "semi-traditional" life but her parents have lived a traditional life. She then begins discussing her birth. She was born in the bush at Warakurna, which she explains is a part of Ngaatjatjarra country. In Ngaatjatjarra culture there is a difference between your home and where you are born. You can be born somewhere, but your home is where your umbilical cord falls off. The authors' parents would move on ceremonial time, so her umbilical cord did not fall off where she was born but rather somewhere else. However, she does not know the name of the place her umbilical cord fell off; nonetheless she considers that place her home.

The author's parents were victims of biocolonialism, for the Commonwealth

Scientific and Industrial Research Organization forced them in fridges to see how long they could last in the cold. Additionally, her parents' sweat was collected through tying plastic bags to the top of their arms and forcing them to run up and down the road. The whole reason her parents and others were tested is so a book could be written about how such families survive the extreme cold and heat of their environment. Her parents never thought they were mistreated. Instead, they laughed and saw "whitefellas" as stupid.

Another instance of colonialism the author mentions is when the police made sure Aboriginal children went to school. She explains that the "half-caste" children, which are also known as the "Stolen Generation," were taken from the reserves to be trained in cities, and that the full-blooded Aboriginals were left on the reserve and had to stay in a hostels while attending school in Leonora. However, the author's family moved a year later to Wiluna and the author had to attend school in Karalundi, which was run by Seventh Day Adventists. Here all the teachers spoke and taught in English.

Later in the text, the author discusses working as a translator working for the Institute of Aboriginal Development. She was asked to translate English into Pintupi-Luritja or Pitjantjatjarra. These languages' dialects are closely related to the author's native Ngaatjatjarra. The author also taught her native language to students in France.

Pictures from My Memory: My Story as a Ngaatjatjarra Woman is a prime example of identity constructed through a double consciousness. The author's "semi-traditional" life is reflective of this. The glossary is helpful, but footnotes along the way would have been better, so that the reader would not have to flip around. Nevertheless, this book offers valuable information on language and its importance to identity.

SHANNON SPEARS is a Ph.D. student in American studies at the University of Kansas.

KEVIN HOOPER

The Life of William Apess, Pequot
by Philip F. Gura
University of North Carolina Press, 2015

IN THIS CAPTIVATING NEW WORK, Philip F. Gura provides a "straightforward account" of the life and experiences of William Apess (xvi). Gura's narrative is exceedingly well written, and he convincingly argues that scholars should understand Apess as not only a Native American intellectual or a religious figure, but also as an important nineteenth-century reformer. In comparing Apess's influence to that of other reformers, including William Lloyd Garrison, David Walker, and Elizabeth Cady Stanton, Gura affirms that "Apess stood both with this cohort and yet apart and above" as he advocated for Native rights (xiv). Like many of his contemporaries, Apess recognized that the United States was plagued by incessant racial inequality and an overt racism that severely restricted the rights of both Native Americans and African Americans living within it. However, unlike William Lloyd Garrison, who rejected Christianity for its supposed defense of slavery, Apess believed that "Christianity provided Native Americans a set of arguments through which to criticize American society" (47). He used Christianity as a means to call for racial equality and insisted that God did not consider whites an exalted race. Instead, Apess believed that "the Indian's soul, too, is immortal, and God is no respecter of persons" (53). Therefore, Apess reasoned that any attempts to restrict Native Americans or African Americans because of their race was not only fundamentally wrong, but also unchristian.

In addition to challenging the strong racist undertones in nineteenth-century America, William Apess recognized that "the physical and psychological oppression that he knew linked him to all Native Americans" (71). An advocate for all of America's Native peoples, not merely his Pequot brethren, Apess traced the "Puritan legacy," or the attempted subjugation of Native peoples by Euro-Americans—often through acts of violence in an effort to acquire their lands—from the Pequot War through to the experiences of the Mashpee and Cherokee peoples during his own lifetime. Consequently, Gura skillfully connects Apess's work in New England and the Northeast more generally to a larger current of reform that transcended geographical, ideological, religious, and racial boundaries.

Gura's *Life of William Apess* is much more than a biographical sketch of Apess's life. Although the work has the feel of a biography, it often reads like a social history. By placing Apess within a broader reform movement, Gura sheds light on the complicated and conflicted nature of nineteenth-century American society, particularly in relation to issues of race and citizenship. As a result, although Gura aims to offer a "straightforward account" of Apess's life, he delivers far more. While the work is successful in making these fascinating broader connections, it leaves the reader wanting more background and content. Nonetheless, one must remember that the book's emphasis is on Apess's life and thus is not a detailed general survey of nineteenth-century America. Readers can find a thorough notes section and selected bibliography at the end of the work that should satisfy those looking for historical or historiographical detours. Gura's work is highly recommended to all, but scholars specializing in literary history, Native American history, or the history of the nineteenth-century United States more broadly will find it of particular merit.

KEVIN HOOPER is a graduate student at the University of Oklahoma.

MELANIE VASSELIN

*Rivers of Sand: Creek Indian Emigration, Relocation, and Ethnic Cleansing
    in the American South*
by Christopher D. Haveman
University of Nebraska Press, 2016

IN THIS BOOK Haveman offers a thorough and critical investigation of the policies, processes, and effects of the ethnic cleansing of the Creek Indian people
through removals from the Southeastern U.S. to Oklahoma in the 1820s to
1840s. This centers on the experiences of Creek people, recounted in their
own words, and evidenced by a diverse range of sources.

With many travelers' accounts, Haveman uses the external gaze to reveal
manifest injustice writ large as well as the particular sufferings of Creek people through specific observations and encounters. Perspectives of government officials and their associates are included, and interestingly the views
of those executing the removal policies often corroborate the accounts of
the Creek people. This book is refreshingly free from the deeply problematic
trope of portraying Indigenous people as passive victims of government policy. Instead, many instances of Creek peoples' consternation are cited, and
their acts of political and legal resistance emphasized. The reader's attention
is drawn to appeals to federal politicians and the legal justice system in attempts to address their concerns, and the book ends with an emphasis on the
endurance and resilience of the Creek people in maintaining and upholding
their culture despite multifaceted attempts to eradicate them.

Haveman does not shy away from describing conflict between federal or
state governments and the Creek people or between Creeks and other Indigenous groups. Perhaps most interesting is the close attention paid to social
stratification within Creek society itself. He is not only cognizant of differences between Upper and Lower Creeks, but he delves deeper into individual communities as well as disparities in wealth and social standing. This
achieves a more holistic portrayal of nineteenth-century Creek society and
exposes differential effects of these policies on social groups within Creek
society and diverse reactions to these, from early voluntary migration by
the McIntosh party to those who migrated decades after the majority of the
population.

This is accomplished through explanations of laws, treaties, and the policy
contexts from which these emerged, combined with a focus on the minutiae
of experiences of removal. Many of these details recount the horrors of illness
and death encountered along the journeys west and after arrival. Indeed,

the book opens with an individual's narrative tracing that of his people. This typifies Haveman's writing, which continually returns to the experiences of individuals and widens out to explore the general trend or underlying occurrences of which these form a part. In so doing, he explores dissenting views and the myriad effects on different social groupings. Part of this comprehensive approach involves exposing some of the more difficult facts to grapple with, such as Creek re-creation of racial hierarchies, endorsement of slavery, and conflicts between certain leaders. Yet even when confronting unpleasant aspects of Creek life at the time, such as problems of alcoholism and acts of violence, close attention is paid to the context in which these emerged and the factors which enabled them, whether these were explicit policies or laws, or effects of government action or inaction, thus painting a nuanced picture.

Haveman acutely observes the backdrop against which these events took place, including the laws passed by Andrew Jackson, the political context, and, often most important, the practical execution of these laws and policies in particular circumstances. The heterogeneity of the people portrayed and details of their journey, from changes in their diet while traveling to the property they transported west, assist in making this history engaging to read. *Rivers of Sand* does not merely recount a chronology of legal and political developments, but discusses their effects on Creek society, culture, and individual lives.

This includes the roles of white settlers and contractors employed to facilitate the migration in contributing to Creek suffering, with governmental complicity and even endorsement. Maps complement the stories of individuals on these journeys, exposing not just a loss of geographic territory but the further psychological and physical harm to the Creeks caused by the process of relocation and continued separation from their territory. This is reflected in the book's title, which highlights the self-contradictory identity of a displaced people.

Through this comprehensive assessment of nineteenth-century Creek removal policy, Haveman exposes various methods of ethnic cleansing ranging from explicit laws, through manipulative treaties, to the push and pull of economic factors, enacted through various agents—all the while retaining a focus on the plight of Creeks and their continued survival and pride despite the tragic events endured.

MELANIE VASSELIN holds an M.Sci. in human rights from the London School of Economics and Political Science and is strongly interested in Indigenous rights.

BENJAMIN L. PÉREZ

Sacred Violence in Early America
by Susan Juster
University of Pennsylvania Press, 2016

DESPITE WHAT THE PROVOCATIVE ILLUSTRATION gracing the book's cover—a depiction of Aztec human sacrifice—would likely lead many potential readers to assume, Susan Juster's *Sacred Violence in Early America* is not an examination or interpretation of pre-, early-, or even post-contact Native American theories and praxes of sacred violence. Rather, Juster's book is a thoughtful and nuanced study of early modern Anglo-American—especially Protestant—understandings and enactments of religiously informed, inspired, and often sanctioned violence—"sacred violence"—directed against perceived religious "others" (including Native Americans, to say nothing of Quakers). Although Bartolomé de las Casas's "Brevísima relación de la destrucción de las Indias" would have been a better choice for the jacket design, beyond the book cover readers will discover the excellent job Juster did contextualizing and historicizing her subject matter: Anglo Americans' colonial-era expressions of sacred violence in the "New World."

Juster's book has four main chapters, each dedicated to digging deeply into an analytically distinct (yet always interrelated, maybe even interdependent) theological/rhetorical paradigm: blood sacrifice, holy war, malediction ("bad speaking"), and iconoclasm. Her study is in the tradition of the *longue durée*: long-term historical structures—in Juster's case, slowly evolving discursive structures—are the foci of her analyses, not "events." From the waning years of the medieval era to the dawn of the American Revolution, always highlighting the profound role that the Reformation played in Western Christians' rethinking of which texts, textures, and contexts best reflect Christianity (and hence best construct Christendom), Juster moves each paradigm through time, demonstrating not only how the discourse surrounding each changes but also that history itself is best understood as an argument for change over time. And just as each chapter's subject becomes more and more abstract, so, too, must she dig ever deeper into the subtleties (and hence ever-shifting complexities) of each paradigm. Indeed, from anxieties over ritual torture, human sacrifice, and anthropophagy (Eucharistic and otherwise) to anxieties over martyrdom and total war (including a new, Protestant version of "holy war" fought for—as well as in—the "New Israel"), from anxieties over blasphemous, heretical, and sacrilegious speech ("sins of the tongue") to anxieties over "icons" and "idols" (including not only Indian burial sites but also, even more disturbing, Indian bodies), Juster shows that just as the past informed each paradigm, so, too, did the ever-changing conditions of the (colonial-era) present reshape each paradigm, often in radical, unexpected, and even contradictory ways; ways that a future John Adams—the "Last Puritan"—would find bewildering.

While reading *Sacred Violence in Early America* one cannot help but draw behavioral parallels between the faith régimes described in Susan Juster's book and today's Taliban (or even ISIS). But Juster's work is a deep cultural history of the theology of violence, especially in the context of colonial-era English America, not an anti-religion polemic à la Sam Harris (nor a pro-religion apologetic à la Karen Armstrong). Juster's work is an instructive example of research rigor, as well as an impressive exegesis of past discursive practices. Her goal is to help readers understand, not judge, past actions that we in the present rightly find upsetting. (The poet Nick Piombino's words are instructive here: "It is intelligent to despise stupidity, yet even more intelligent to comprehend it.") If one is looking for a history book in the vein of Howard Zinn, then this book will disappoint; again, Juster's work is a cultural history of sacred violence, not a grab bag from which to cherry-pick—to decontextualize—moments and events from the past to advance current culture wars and political agendas. True, academics devoid of pragmatics violates—even offends—many Native American studies scholars' activist ethos. But somewhere between academic pastism and activist presentism—somewhere between L. P. Hartley's "The past is a foreign country; they do things differently there" and William Faulkner's "The past is never dead; it's not even past"—is an understanding of history that is as honest as it is useful. Indeed, if one is interested in acquiring a deeply nuanced understanding of the complexity—as well as centrality—of Indian diabolism in colonial apologetics (and, by extension, a deeper understanding of those disquieting echoes of that past in our present), then *Sacred Violence in Early America* is indeed worth reading.

BENJAMIN L. PÉREZ is a faculty member at the College of the Marshall Islands.

REBECCA MACKLIN

Understanding Louise Erdrich
by Seema Kurup
University of South Carolina Press, 2015

THE INCLUSION OF Louise Erdrich in the "Understanding Contemporary American Literature" series attests to her position as one of the most important American authors writing today. Though fans and scholars of Erdrich's work would argue this has been the case since she won the 1984 National Book Critics Circle Award with her debut novel, *Love Medicine*, this position was irrefutably cemented when she won the Library of Congress Prize for American Fiction in 2015.

Kurup's aim here is to provide an introduction to Erdrich's writing, and she succeeds in giving a fairly holistic overview. This book places Erdrich's work into the context of her life, upbringing, and cultural identity, which is ultimately framed in the context of Erdrich's Ojibwe heritage. This is a challenging task to undertake in a short text—indeed, just over one hundred pages—for any author, and particularly so for an author as prolific as Erdrich. Kurup therefore does not attempt to incorporate all of Erdrich's work: rather, she highlights key texts, grouped together by chronology, genre, or theme, and situates them within the context of Erdrich's oeuvre. Yet an ambitious amount of material is covered in a short number of pages. Rather than undertaking an in-depth analysis of each text, Kurup reads her chosen texts through the lens of selected themes: primarily, Ojibwe experiences of settler colonialism, assimilation, and cultural survival. Kurup situates the works within their socio-historic contexts, making this a useful guide to those unfamiliar with the historical experiences of Indigenous peoples under the U.S. government.

Kurup impressively foregrounds connections across Erdrich's oeuvre, arguing that she has "created a literature of place" (6) imbued with the traumatic legacies of settler colonialism and the memories of the Ojibwe. However, by choosing key themes through which to analyze Erdrich's work, some are inevitably omitted. Viewing Erdrich through this lens means that some of the most exciting and challenging elements of her work are overlooked—particularly her engagements with gender and sexuality. Considering the series title, it is also somewhat surprising that Kurup does little to position Erdrich in relation to her literary influences and a broader literary tradition. In addition, it would be interesting to see more focus on Erdrich's work in the context of contemporary issues faced by Indigenous people in North

America. There are brief moments of illumination in which Kurup discusses Erdrich's work in relation to contemporary concerns, such as climate change and global capitalism, but the discussion primarily focuses on the settler-colonial history that informs Erdrich's writing.

Though essential for an introductory text, much of the material Kurup includes in the first few chapters has been covered elsewhere. For example, details of the "Silko-Erdrich controversy," as it has become known, are included in most accounts of Erdrich's work. The most interesting sections, and opportunities for real insight, come in the later chapters focused on Erdrich's more recent novels, nonfiction, her children's series, and her poetry—all of which have, thus far, received comparatively little critical engagement. Kurup's core argument is that all of Erdrich's works should be read together—and her analysis of Erdrich's poetry and children's books alongside her more critically received works is convincing. The chapter on Erdrich's Birchbark House series is particularly engaging, in which Kurup argues that the inherently political nature of Erdrich's writing transcends genre and form. Focusing on her radical use of Ojibwe language in these books, which "preserves and records the language . . . for generations to come" (74), Kurup observes that "language is inextricably tied to history and place for the Ojibwe; losing it could have devastating consequences" (75). The focus on Erdrich's poetry, too, offers valuable insight. Kurup's analysis of the 1984 poem "Runaways," which highlights the neglected histories of the residential boarding school system, is remarkably prescient in light of Erdrich's most recent novel, *LaRose* (2016). Kurup's analysis of this poem, written at the start of Erdrich's career, resonates with the novel's focus on the traumatic legacies of the schools and the disruptive, de-colonial power of dreams. The children in the boarding school, she suggests, "are seemingly not colonized in the space of their dreams; they enjoy a subconscious freedom there. Only their bodies are subjected to systematic assimilation" (93–94).

Taking into account its short length, this book accomplishes an extraordinary level of depth and varied analysis within its pages. Kurup's inclusion of Erdrich's lesser-explored works alongside analysis of established novels offers real insight. For any readers wishing to learn more about Erdrich's oeuvre—and particularly how Native American history informs her writing—this book is a valuable point of entry.

REBECCA MACKLIN is a Ph.D. candidate in comparative literature at the University of Leeds and a 2017–18 Fulbright scholar at Cornell University.

NICK ESTES

Red Bird, Red Power: The Life and Legacy of Zitkala-Ša
by Tadeusz Lewandowski
University of Oklahoma Press, 2016

NÉE GERTRUDE SIMMONS in 1876 and assuming the Dakota nom de plume Zitkala-Ša (or Red Bird) in the early 1900s, Zitkala-Ša is the most profound and underrated American Indian intellectual of her generation. Scholars have often misunderstood this Yankton Sioux poet, musician, educator, critic, and activist as an assimilationist. Tadeusz Lewandowski's *Red Bird, Red Power: The Life and Legacy of Zitkala-Ša* wades into the debate arguing against "assimilation" and "liminal" categorizations. Zitkala-Ša was neither an assimilationist like many of her "Red Progressive" colleagues nor was she a tragic victim of the "two worlds" paradigm, the failing to negotiate white and Indigenous realities. As the title of the book suggests, Zitkala-Ša should instead be understood as "a forerunner to Red Power" because she advocated "Indian cultural renewal and political independence" at a time when the American Indian population was at its lowest and thought to be vanishing into the wilderness of history (16).

Although the product of a Quaker education herself, Zitkala-Ša first gained notoriety with a series of autobiographical stories published in the *Atlantic Monthly* that denounced the violent church- and government-run Indian boarding school system. She was not opposed to Indian education, and she even took a teaching position at the infamous Carlisle Indian School. The problem was the way education was used to annihilate American Indian cultures, a criticism that drew ire from her mentor and employer Richard Pratt. While critical of boarding school education, her stories also affirmed the superiority American Indian culture, specifically of the Sioux. This message, however, was lost on white society, who "ignored or criticized" Zitkala-Ša and cast her as a "civilized savage" (44). This view plagued her for the rest of her career.

The battleground was not confined to literary circles. Zitkala-Ša spent years on the Uintah reservation in Utah, where she organized community self-help groups. The work led her to join the ranks of the "Red Progressives," a generation of American Indian intellectuals and professionals that founded the Society of American Indians (SAI) in 1911. SAI held diverse views on assimilation and peyote use but generally advocated for American Indian citizenship, education, and the abolition of the Indian Bureau. Zitkala-Ša, who had by then converted to Catholicism, adamantly opposed assimilation and peyote use and advocated for full citizenship. Her peyote position oscillated between Christian temperance and a perception that the peyote priests (all older men) preyed on young women, children, and the vulnerable, which occurred but not with great frequency. The citizenship question was pragmatic. How could American Indians protect tribal lands and hold the government accountable if they possessed no rights under law? Citizenship became a further sticking point during World War I, as American Indians enlisted in large numbers.

Zitkala-Ša's views on peyote and citizenship mar her legacy. But she was more forward-thinking. For example, Zitkala-Ša pushed SAI to seek international representation at the 1919 Paris Peace Conference to advance American Indian citizenship and self-determination. She tried to reshape the SAI top-down style of organizing to one where each tribe could form its own SAI chapter. Under this structure, she believed SAI would eventually replace the Indian Bureau. Neither measure came to pass. Frustrated that SAI failed as a Progressive Era vehicle of reform, Zitkala-Ša returned to community organizing and formed the National Council of American Indians in 1926. She worked tirelessly on many fronts to advance American Indian rights, from the Osage oil boom, to the Sioux Black Hills land claim, to legal rights for California Indians. The grueling pace caused both financial and physical exhaustion, leading to her death in 1938.

To her contemporaries Zitkala-Ša was an exotic figure, a "civilized savage." In reality, she was a firebrand Indigenous nationalist and a fierce advocate. Commenting on her own legacy she said, "They all want to know about me, but I would rather they would ask about the Indians" (173). Lewandowski argues that we need to know more about Zitkala-Ša *and* the Indians. Indeed, Zitkala-Ša was a forerunner to Red Power. But she was also a product of her time. More important, she is a profound testament to the existence of a historical Indigenous radical tradition. Denying over-coded binaries of assimilation, her legacy begs us to understand early twentieth-century intellectuals like her as part of a longer tradition of Indigenous resistance.

NICK ESTES (KUL WICASA) is a doctoral candidate in American studies at the University of New Mexico.

KELLY WISECUP

Imprints: The Pokagon Band of Potawatomi Indians
  and the City of Chicago
by John N. Low
Michigan State University Press, 2016

IN *IMPRINTS* JOHN N. LOW offers a history of how the Pokagon Band of Potawatomi Indians and the city of Chicago influenced—or made imprints on—each other, from the precolonial Potawatomi presence in the region to the present. In chapters that focus on Potawatomi leaders such as Leopold Pokagon and his son Simon Pokagon, Michael B. Williams, and Leroy Wesaw alongside Chicago's efforts to eliminate Potawatomi people from its land and memory, Low details the creative ways the Pokagon Band resisted assimilation and elimination. While the 1833 Treaty of Chicago forced many Potawatomi people to relocate west of the Mississippi, the Pokagon Band retained a land base in Michigan. Tribal leader Leopold Pokagon negotiated an amendment that allowed his band to remain on land he had been granted by the federal government. In such contexts of removal, assimilation, and cultural erasure, the Pokagon Band maintained a relationship with Chicago. As Low shows, Pokagon Band members felt a great deal of ambivalence toward the city, given its history of colonialism, but they engaged with the city nonetheless. They transformed what were often attempts to misremember or forget Chicago's relations with Potawatomi people into opportunities to exercise agency over representations of their people and to build inter- and intra-tribal relations. As a result, the Potawatomi shaped the city's history and physical landscape, as Low details in six chapters and several appendices. The book traces Potawatomi imprints in public events, community events, legal land claims, art, writing, and performance.

Key to Potawatomi imprints is what Low calls "re-collection": strategies of "reengaging with the technology and material culture of the past . . . to support individual and community identity as indigenous peoples" (xiv) and to "reconnect . . . the past to the present and to the future" (9). In the 1960s, recollection took the form of establishing canoe clubs with the American Indian Center, clubs that strengthened community identity. In the 2000s band members contributed to public art that represented the long history of Native people in Chicago, and they repeatedly engaged in debates about how the city memorialized the Battle of Fort Dearborn (often called a massacre in popular and official publications). Re-collection, Low details, also meant building wigwams in public spaces and filing legal claims to lakefill (areas submerged under Lake Michigan when treaties were signed but later filled in and thus not part of land the Potawatomi ceded to the United States). As these examples suggest, material culture is a crucial focus of Low's study: as he puts it, the "Pokagon Potawatomi constructed monuments, when and where they could, in Chicago" (xiv). Low takes a capacious view of the term "monument," reading books, legal cases, speeches, and acts of everyday life as strategies with which the Pokagon Potawatomi erected physical and intellectual signs of their presence. Low pairs his focus on monuments and material culture with an archive composed of oral histories, interviews, his own experiences and insights as a Pokagon Potawatomi band member, and archival research. In doing so, he offers new interpretations of histories and places that might appear wholly under settler control by showing how strategic Potawatomi participation could turn such sites to tribal uses.

Imprints joins recent scholarship that has revised the relations between Native people and urban contexts, and Low's study is a welcome addition to books by Susan Lobo, Andrew Needham, Reyna K. Ramirez, and Coll Thrush. It adds a new methodological focus to such studies by considering tribal identity as well as geographic location as key frameworks. While at times the focus on the Pokagon Band obscures the fact that, thanks to the U.S. relocation policy of the 1950s and 1960s people from many tribal affiliations call Chicago home, Low's band-specific focus powerfully challenges assumptions—still alive and well in Chicago today—that all Native people were removed from Chicago and its region in 1833. Finally, Low's book contributes to recent studies of the "Indigenous Midwest," such as the special issue of the Middle West Review edited by Doug Kiel and James F. Brooks, by showing just how deeply Potawatomi and urban histories are intertwined. Imprints is a useful, engaging, and accessible book, one of great value for those interested in urban histories, the Midwest and Chicago, memory studies, and the Potawatomi.

KELLY WISECUP is an assistant professor in the English Department at Northwestern University.

NOENOE K. SILVA

The Learned Ones: Nahua Intellectuals in Postconquest Mexico
by Kelly S. McDonough
University of Arizona Press, 2014

KELLY MCDONOUGH'S *The Learned Ones: Nahua Intellectuals in Postconquest Mexico* is a fascinating account and analysis of Nahua intellectuals from the early sixteenth century to the present. All are writers whose works are mainly in the Nahuatl language. The book begins with a quote from a contemporary student who has learned his Nahua ancestors wrote: "So all this time they were lying to us, the schoolteachers. They said we were stupid *burrohmeh*, nothing but donkeys. I guess they were wrong" (3). This moment when an Indigenous person breaks through the mental wall created by the systematic erasure of their own history is the reason why many academics (including me) are working on Indigenous intellectual histories. Reconstructing this knowledge of the brilliance and skill of our ancestors for our peoples is one of the ways we can recover from the cultural bombs of colonialism (see, for instance, Ngugi Wa Thiong'o's *Decolonising the Mind: The Politics of Language in African Literature*). The construction of the divide between savagery and civilization as alphabetic writing justified European colonialism for the colonizers, and the subsequent processes of historiography and settler colonialism have hidden from view the talents of Indigenous peoples in not only their own modes of writing, but the European alphabetic system as well. McDonough's book demonstrates the breadth and depth of the history of Nahuatl alphabetic writing while educating us in the history of the Nahua people along the way. McDonough's methodology importantly includes collaboration and the return of knowledge to the Nahua communities. The book makes substantial contributions in the areas of Indigenous history, Indigenous language revitalization, Nahuatl language and contemporary politics, and Indigenous research methodologies.

Chapter 1 tells the story of Antonio del Rincón, "the first Indigenous person in the Americas to write a grammar of his own language" and "perhaps the only Indigenous man ordained by the Jesuits in the early colonial period" (34). Rincón contributed to the colonization of his people through assisting the evangelical project by teaching other priests the Nahuatl language, but he also made substantial intellectual contributions.

Don Juan Buenaventura Zapata y Mendoza, "the author/compiler of one of the richest extant Nahuatl-language historical annals of the altepetl (city/state) of Tlaxcala" (63), is the focus of chapter 2. Zapata's written work "is a rich testament to Indigenous survival, cultural pride, and political finesse in times of crisis and change" (82).

Chapter 3 introduces the reader to the work of the nineteenth-century professor of law and Nahuatl and Otomí languages Faustino Galicia Chimapopoca. He transcribed and translated "scores of colonial-period Nahuatl texts" and authored many religious works in both Nahuatl and Spanish. His work has been critiqued as flawed and, as a result, "nearly erased from historical memory" (115), but McDonough persuades us that all interested in the survival of Nahuatl and the record of writing in it owe him gratitude for his acts to preserve the archive.

Chapters 4 and 5 introduce us to two twentieth-century Nahua intellectuals, Doña Luz Jiménez and Ildefonso Maya Hernández. Jiménez's visage has become an icon of Mexico, as she modeled for the likes of Diego Rivera and Jean Charlot, but here McDonough productively reverses the gaze and exchanges the medium (paraphrasing her words) as she analyzes Jiménez's testimonial writings and short stories. The stories constitute perhaps the only "published Nahuatl-language texts that narrate the firsthand experience of assimilative education for Indians in early twentieth-century Mexico" (123). Hernández was an educator, playwright, artist, and activist whose work depicts "the challenges faced by Indigenous people in Mexico today" (160). Some of the most interesting of Hernández's works are bilingual twentieth-century codices in the style of his ancestors. McDonough explains they were "a move to recover and redesign Indigenous discursive and material communication tools" (189).

Overall, this detailed examination of Nahua writing from the sixteenth century to the present is an extended and powerful argument for Indigenous language perpetuation and revitalization. The book reveals that the value of Indigenous languages is not (only) about the beauty of and knowledge contained in our languages that are pleasurable or useful for today but also the ability of Indigenous peoples to create full lives for ourselves.

The book is suitable for both undergraduate and graduate courses, as McDonough clearly contextualizes everything and refrains from too much academic jargon. I have used it in a graduate Indigenous theory course to good effect. This work is a treasure and inspiration for anyone interested in Indigenous histories or languages.

NOENOE K. SILVA (KANAKA HAWAI‘I) is professor of Indigenous politics and Hawaiian language at the University of Hawai‘i at Mānoa.

AIMEE E. CARBAUGH

Ancestral Mounds: Vitality and Volatility of Native America
by Jay Miller
University of Nebraska Press, 2015

EARTHEN MOUNDS dot the landscape of the eastern half of North America, from Oklahoma to the Atlantic Ocean. These mounds are testaments to the interaction between humans and their environment, a means for balancing the relationship of people with the cosmos. Many of these earthworks are preserved on lands belonging to Native tribes, on private land, as protected historical sites, or have been destroyed. The building of mounds, which range in size from low earthen rises to massive construction projects soaring one hundred feet toward the sky, is rarely discussed outside Indigenous communities or academia. Are mounds only a remnant of the past? Do mounds still hold meaning for Indigenous communities today? How have historical events affected the relationship between Native peoples and mounds? Why may mounds be important?

Jay Miller, in his book *Ancestral Mounds*, addresses these questions by examining the historical and current understanding of North American mounds, primarily focusing on the Southeast. Throughout the book Miller relies on ethnographic descriptions of mound construction and their use, written by explorers, missionaries, naturalists, anthropologists, archaeologists, ethnographers, and linguists. A brief historical overview of the use of mounds is provided in chapter 2 for the Chicora, Western Chitimachas, Atakapa, Chickasaw, Natchez, Delaware, and Tutelo tribes. The construction and significance of the different types of mounds throughout the Southeast is also covered. Miller provides ethnographic examples of contemporary Native communities' mounding practices, including the cyclical process of renewal through burning and rebuilding. He also addresses how these present-day practices help in the interpretation of archaeological excavations of mounds.

Ancestral Mounds touches on the traumatic historical events endured by Indigenous groups in North America with examples focusing on the Southeast. Disease devastated Indigenous populations, causing different communities to merge. This was followed by the forced removal of many Native groups from their homelands, resulting in further consolidation. In being forced to move, these communities left behind their ancestral mounds, which had kept them safe and had weighed down the shifting earth. They took soil with them from their mounds in order to establish new mounds, thus providing a connection to their ancestral lands. This series of events has shaped the tribes present in the Southeast today.

Miller is adamant that readers understand how mounds continue to provide a source of vitality for Indigenous communities. As an example, he describes the Green Corn Ceremony of the Seminole, along with ethnographic accounts of historical ceremonial practices for several Creek communities. Mounds are part of the ceremonial landscape, helping to create a sacred space where the ceremonies are carried out, and they are added to and revitalized through mounding, song, and dance. The survival of the mounds and the Green Corn Ceremony demonstrates the importance and longevity of these practices in North America, a means for community renewal and for maintaining balance in the cosmos.

Ancestral Mounds is an introductory text on the role of earthen mounds in Indigenous communities. Miller offers readers brief glimpses into the historical and contemporary understanding of numerous Indigenous communities in relation to their practices and beliefs surrounding mounds. The pre-contact evidence presented is sparse, with the bulk of the interpretation coming from ethnographic descriptions gathered since the arrival of Europeans. Throughout the book, Miller calls attention to how the past can inform the present and vice versa, along with implementing a cross disciplinary approach to research.

While *Ancestral Mounds* incorporates discussions of pre-contact North America and of archaeological excavations, the archaeological studies presented are not explored in sufficient detail. The majority of the sources cited are outdated, pre-2000, and do not reflect the current theoretical approaches. More recent archaeological interpretations of sites, such as Cahokia, incorporate ethnographic studies in their research on mounds and ceremonial sites. Recognizing the continuity through time of different aspects of ceremonial practices is part of archaeological research, as is acknowledging the significance of mounds for contemporary Indigenous communities.

As one aspect of the Indigenous ceremonial landscape, earthen mounds are crucial for ensuring the safety of humans in an unstable universe. Their presence on the landscape demonstrates the longevity of Native peoples in eastern North America. *Ancestral Mounds* provides us with the continuity through time of Indigenous ceremonial practices and addresses the continued struggle by Indigenous communities for recognition of their importance.

AIMEE E. CARBAUGH is a Ph.D. student in anthropology at the University of Illinois at Urbana—Champaign.

MARÍA JOSEFINA SALDAÑA-PORTILLO

*Stand Up and Fight: Participatory Indigenismo, Populism,
    and Mobilization in Mexico, 1970–1984*
by María L. O. Muñoz
University of Arizona Press, 2016

IN *STAND UP AND FIGHT*, María L. O. Muñoz recuperates the history of Mexico's 1975 First National Congress of Indigenous Peoples and the subsequent National Council of Indigenous Peoples from the perspective of the bilingual indigenous activists who organized both. Muñoz conducted extensive interviews with the principal organizers and gained rare access to their personal correspondence and archives. As a consequence, she presents the reader with an original and field-changing book. The 1975 First National Congress is a watershed event in the Mexican history; however, historians, political theorists, and anthropologists have adhered to a simplistic analysis of the Congress (and the Council) as orchestrated by the Mexican state for the purposes of refurbishing the tarnished repututation of the Institutional Revolutionary Party (the PRI, as known in Spanish) after the repression of the 1968 student and guerrilla movements. Indeed, President Luis Echevarría (1970–76), believed to have ordered the 1968 Tlatelolco student massacre as Interior Secretary, ran on a platform of returning to revolutionary populism, including a recommitment to "participatory indigenismo" as the means of addressing indigenous peoples' socioeconomic needs. Thus the indigenous activists who worked with Echevarría's administration to organize the Congress and the Council have been dismissed by scholars as at best dupes, and at worse sellouts who willingly whitewashed the reputation of an assassin.

Muñoz's analytical perspective exposes this representation of the indigenous activists for what it is, at best mestizo condescension, at worse a racist denial of indigenous agency. Instead, Muñoz convincingly argues that "bilingual promoters" (as the indigenous activists are called) maneuvered within the "field of force" between the ruling elite and the subaltern to the advantage of indigenous communities. Rather than portray them as manipulated by forces beyond their control, Muñoz documents the manner in which bilingual promoters used their unique position as cultural and linguistic mediators to catapult indigenous peoples onto the national political stage, to forge a unified indigenous identity from the diversity of indigenous peoples, and to demand revolutionary redress for their economic marginalization and political exclusion. More than seventy-five regional indigenous congresses took place leading up to First National Congress, and Muñoz reconstructs the roles played by bilingual promoters in those regional conferences by retracing their travels across the entire country, outlining the specific dialogues and conflicts theses bilingual promoters had with regional indigenous leaders, as well as restaging the power plays made by local and state officials opposed to the Congress and participatory indigenismo. In Muñoz's invaluable historical reconstruction of events, she is as frank about the failures of bilingual promoters as she is laudatory in reevaluating their successful efforts at controlling the field of force. With the Congress and the Council, these bilingual promoters created a national indigenous organization capable of representing indigenous peoples as full Mexican citizens who nevertheless retained rights and privileges as the original inhabitants of Mexico. Yet, as Muñoz amply documents, constructing this singular vision of a national indigenous political organization at times clashed with indigenous communities who had other forms of governance they wanted to preserve, or who preferred to engage with local "fields of force" rather than intervene at the national level. All this Muñoz reconstructs with unflinching detail, including the manner in which indigenous leaders in the regional conferences were manipulated by regional government agents from the National Peasant Confederation (CNC) intent on derailing the National Congress, even though Echevarría had ordered the CNC to assist in its organization.

This is another much-needed correction to the historiography of the Congress and the Council. Muñoz reconstructs the protracted struggle by which the bilingual promoters wrenched control of the Congress from the CNC by appealing directly and repeatedly to Echevarría's inner circle, demonstrating their political expertise in operating in the field of force. This success enabled an indigenous identity to emerge as separate and apart from peasant identity, a determining factor in enabling a national appeal for indigenous rights. While the Congress and the Council were superseded by indigenous organizations and forums free of state control, Muñoz admirably demonstrates the strategically important role of the Congress and Council in creating the political space for independent groups to thrive. Moreover, her analysis foregrounds the political agency in the national field of force exerted not only by the bilingual promoters, but also by the thousands of indigenous representatives, and hundreds of indigenous communities, that participated in the years-long processes that culminated in the Congress and the Council. *Stand Up and Fight* is an invaluable restoration of a key moment in the political history of indigenous peoples in twentieth-century Mexico.

MARÍA JOSEFINA SALDAÑA-PORTILLO is a professor in the Department of Social and Cultural Analysis at New York University.

EMILIO DEL VALLE ESCALANTE

Indian Given: Racial Geographies across Mexico and the United States
by Maria Josefina Saldaña-Portillo
Duke University Press, 2016

MARIA JOSEFINA SALDAÑA-PORTILLO'S *Indian Given* examines the racial geography formations that have taken place in what is today Mexico and the United States since Spanish and British colonialist incursions. It interrogates the representations of Indians by settlers and their descendants in the archives of colonial conquest and other textualities that have contributed to formation of national identities in Mexico and the United States. The representations of the "Indio" and "Indian," it is argued, served to secure white/criollo-mestizo supremacy by justifying and facilitating the conquest of Indigenous territories. In turn, these representations have created new perceptions of the landscape and its people, especially on the border. The title of the book plays on the derogatory term "Indian giver"—someone who takes back something they have willingly given or sold—in order to challenge how and why the Spanish and the British colonial enterprises produced dissimilar racial geographies that led to "two distinct but complicit genealogies of Indian difference as produced in colonial and national geographies" (8).

The book is divided into an introduction, five chapters, and a coda. In chapter 1 Saldaña-Portillo concentrates on the Spanish and British invaders' juridical encounters with Indigeneity. She first discusses the question of Indigenous humanity and the "just" methods of "New World" conquest as these emerge in the debates between Fray Bartolomé de las Casas and Juan Ginés de Sepúlveda between 1550 and 1552. In the second part of the chapter she focuses on the British Crown's Proclamation of 1763, which consequently positioned the elites from the thirteen colonies as authorities on Indigenous character and a remapping of the "new" territories. Chapter 2 analyzes documents from the Spanish colonial archive on settlement and war in Texas, and compares them to the film *No Country for Old Men* to distinguish the hetero-temporal function of the "Indio Bárbaro" from early conquest to the war on terror. The first section focuses on Antonio Ladrón de Guevara's 1738 petition to the Spanish Crown to settle and populate what is today Texas. Saldaña-Portillo then analyzes a set of letters that discuss the 1758–59 Comanche attacks on the San Sabá presidio and mission in Texas. The chapter closes with *No Country for Old Men* to show "the transnational legacy of Spanish and Anglo-American racial graphing of the Southwest" (69). Chapter 3 examines the "nationalist transformations of the geography of the 'frontier'" (109) by discussing the ideas of the "Indio Bárbaro" employed to differentiate Apaches and Comanches who refused to embrace "mestizaje" (racial mixing) or were pushed to reservations in the newly annexed territories of the U.S. Southwest. The chapter compares and contrasts the Treaty of Guadalupe de Hidalgo and nineteenth-century Mexican scalping laws with Américo Paredes's novel *George Washington Gomez*. Chapter 4 examines the early civil rights campaigns of Mexican and Mexican Americans in the Southwest to end segregation in schools between 1896 and 1954. Saldaña-Portillo analyzes, among other legal cases, *Mendez v. Westminster*, *United States v. Lucero*, and *Hernandez v. Texas* and compares them to personal letters and public speeches of the Mexican American activists who participated in debates about U.S. naturalization. Chapter 5 unravels the "problematic racial coordinates of Aztlan" (197) through an analysis of the works of the Chicano activist, journalist and lawyer Oscar Zeta Acosta. Saldaña-Portillo is interested in showing how Chicanas/os articulate the idea of Aztlan through a melancholic and frenzied representation that incorporates a "lost Indigeneity" while at the same time justifies its Chicana/o presence in Indigenous territories. The first section of the chapter focuses on Acosta's journalism and legal trials, and the second on *The Autobiography of a Brown Buffalo*.

Indian Given closes with "The Afterlives of the Indio Bárbaro," which invokes this racial identity construction to signal its contemporary relevance in Mexico and the United States. The idea of the "Indio Bárbaro" is associated with the "Muslim" and "narco" terrorists invoked by Mexican president Felipe Calderón and U.S. president Barack Obama: "The old racial geography of the borderlands informs the new, with the indio bárbaro as a simplistic explanation for the economic restructuring brought on both countries by NAFTA and the drug economy it enables." (246).

Indian Given will be of great interest to scholars and university students who explore issues of Indigeneity in Mexico and the United States. Its interdisciplinary inquiry makes an important contribution to the field of Indigenous studies.

EMILIO DEL VALLE ESCALANTE (K'ICHE' MAYA, IXIMULEW) is an associate professor in the Romance Studies Department at the University of North Carolina at Chapel Hill.

JOSEPH BAUERKEMPER

Dream Wheels: A Novel
by Richard Wagamese
Milkweed Editions, 2016

IN MARCH 2017 the world of Native writing lost one of its exceptionally effective and productive storytellers. Even as relatives, friends, and readers mourn the death of Ojibway (Wabaseemoong First Nation) writer Richard Wagamese, the recent reissue of his novel *Dream Wheels* should contribute to the continued growth of his already extensive and well-deserved audience. Originally published in 2006, the book was reissued in 2016 by Milkweed Editions, a Minneapolis-based nonprofit publisher and co-constituent of the Open Book literary arts center. Following two plotlines that organically merge, *Dream Wheels* tells the stories of a catastrophically injured Ojibway—Sioux rodeo cowboy and a traumatized African American mother and son enduring a string of abusive relationships and navigating the juvenile corrections system. On the cusp of attaining the All-Around Cowboy championship, gifted rodeo rider Joe Willie Wolfchild is injured during a bull ride and must face a life beyond rodeo with drastically limited physical capacities. Claire Hartley is simultaneously straining to extract herself and her son Aiden, who has been imprisoned in association with an attempted robbery, from a cyclical series of abusive relationships. Despite setting shifts from corrals to hospital rooms, suburban sprawl, juvenile prison, and working ranchland, the book consistently reflects the prevalence of land. The novel's groundedness is frequently made explicit through dialog and narration while also remaining as a constant presence even when unmentioned.

Like other works by Wagamese, *Dream Wheels* emphasizes the healing power of land and relationships in its portrayal of abuse of various sorts: physical, sexual, emotional, and alcoholic. While many literary representations of Native peoples depict social dysfunctions such as alcoholism, sexual violence, and physical abuse—and while some of those literary representations acknowledge that dysfunction emanates from and is constitutive of colonialism—*Dream Wheels* makes a conspicuous departure in its own consideration of these phenomena. Within the world of the novel, abuse and dysfunction are quite clearly associated with settler provenance. None of the Native characters in the novel engages in alcohol or substance abuse, and none of them perpetrates or even experiences physical or sexual violence. All characters engaging in alcohol abuse are white, and physical, emotional, and sexual abuse are the exclusive domain of white male perpetrators. Moreover,

Wagamese is not heavy-handed with these representations. The narrator does not, for example, directly remark on the absence of Native alcohol consumption. Nor is there abstract commentary on racialized white violence. The toxicity of settler masculinity and the healthy functionality of Native kinship are instead both organically situated within the novel. While the impact of the former is not at all minimized, the transformative power of the latter is nevertheless more prominent. The kinship traditions maintained, honored, and shared within the novel's Native family are the source and outcome of healing.

The healing process narrated in the book rests within a simple yet robust web of relations. These connections bring together the Wolfchild story and the Hartley story as mutually enabled accounts of recovery. The intersections afford Wagamese several occasions to consider the dynamic nature of living tradition. Whether Ojibway knowledge and protocol, rodeo heritage, or black and Native cowboy histories that defy stereotypical expectations, *Dream Wheels* consistently returns to the traditions that ground its characters and provide the foundations and resources for living in a good way. Linked to its consideration of tradition, the novel repeatedly addresses the concept of history, primarily when focalized by Claire Hartley. Her yearning to create a usable past for her family's future marks both the early absence of relations and the significance of kinship in her and Aiden's lives—kinship ultimately learned and intertwined with the Wolfchild family.

Even at four hundred pages, *Dream Wheels* is an eminently readable episodic text that moves briskly and firmly holds reader attention from start to finish. This Milkweed reissue brings forth a widely accessible and affordable printing of the novel that should be of particular interest to course instructors at the undergraduate and upper-secondary levels, as well as to academic readers interested in contemporary Ojibwe literature, Indigenous kinship, the North American West, and black—Indian interactions. While many readers will note a few moments in which the novel perhaps too generally references Indian cultural traditions, these references can be and should be linked back to the novel's particular cultural contexts. In any case, the mild challenges that the book would pose to Native American and Indigenous studies teachers are well worth the work the book can do on behalf of students.

JOSEPH BAUERKEMPER is an associate professor of American Indian studies at the University of Minnesota Duluth.

ANNEMARIE McLAREN

A Handful of Sand: The Gurindji Struggle, After the Walk-Off
by Charlie Russell Ward
Monash University Publishing, 2016

IN AUGUST 1966 Vincent Lingiari led two hundred people in a strike off Wave Hill cattle station in the Northern Territory of Australia. Challenging the status quo in which Aboriginal stockmen and their families worked for meager pay and substandard housing despite being vital to the operation of cattle stations in the interior, they left this branch of a multinational conglomerate business to follow a dream: to run a cattle station on their own land. *A Handful of Sand* is about what happened after the walk-off: the currents of Gurindji life from that point onward, and how, when, and why the Gurindji became the focal point—and political football—of Indigenous land rights across Australia.

In a basic sense this is a work of political history. The Wave Hill Walk-Off catalyzed economic change, social and legal debate, and reform. The title itself is drawn from the symbolic moment in which Australian Prime Minister Gough Whitlam poured a handful of soil from Gurindji country into Vincent Lingiara's hands. Yet *A Handful of Sand* is much more than a work of political history. It is committed to charting Gurindji life: the ongoing wear and tear, trials and triumphs, of which the historic granting of a lease, the formation of the Gurindji's own cattle run, and the iconic handful of sand constitute highpoints but not the end of the pulse of Gurindji lives and fortunes.

As the dedication to the realization of the Gurdinji's hopes and dreams foreshadows, Ward, a *kartiya* or white man, has made sure that the people and the places *are* the history as much as, or even more than, the politics and the key events. In a work about a small community and a wider political stage, such detailed portraits are both fitting and compelling. "Sensitivity" is an overused term, but the acuity of Ward's book lies in this and a commitment so great that it cannot shy away from the people and places involved or the rawness of it all. Ward details the human cost of oscillating political fortune as well as other realities: intergenerational conflict, substance abuse, the difficulties of a cash economy, encroaching age and senility, and the issues of translation in policy makers' requirements.

Published on the fiftieth anniversary of the Wave Hill Walk-Off, this book will be an illuminating read for scholars and layman nationally and internationally—aided by helpful maps and a list of terms. For those wanting a firmer grasp of the history of Indigenous land rights in Australia, no finer introduction of the tone, texture, and story could be given, due in large part to Ward's impressive array of interviews. For those interested in the ongoing social and political turbulence for many Indigenous people more generally, this book will also yield rich insights.

ANNEMARIE McLAREN is a doctoral candidate in Aboriginal—colonial history at the Australian National University.

ANTHONY SNETHEN

*Free to Be Mohawk: Indigenous Education at the Akwesasne Freedom
    School*
by Louellyn White
University of Oklahoma Press, 2015

LOUELLYN WHITE'S *Free to Be Mohawk* provides a glimpse into a self-determined school in the Mohawk territory of Akwesasne in northern New York. Born out of the struggle between traditionalists and those who accepted colonial political and social structures, the Akwesasne Freedom School (AFS) was founded on the principals of self-governance, self-sufficiency, language revitalization, and culturally appropriate education. The book weaves together the founding stories and Longhouse tradition of the Haudenosaunee (Iroquois) people, the battle over Mohawk community identity, the struggle for self-determined education, and the revitalization of Kanienke:ha, the Mohawk language. More important, though, *Free to Be Mohawk* illustrates the vast potential for decolonization through self-determined education in a sovereign nation.

White begins the book with a question: What does it mean to be Mohawk? This becomes relevant to her upon the passing of her father, when she begins to question her own identity. The child of a Mohawk father and a white mother, White holds tenuous connections to Akwesasne, but her position as a researcher places her as an outsider. She confronts her insider/outsider positionality early on by asserting that separation of personal and academic life is not necessary; just as she cannot separate her Mohawk heritage from her non-Indigenous heritage, so, too, are her positions as both an insider and an outsider inseparable. Also imperative to her research is the importance of conducting her study in collaboration with, and for the benefit of, the Mohawk people.

The exploration of White's central question begins with an overview of the foundational stories of the Haudenosaunee people. She then relates the founding of the Akwesasne Freedom School, which began due to a standoff between followers of the Longhouse tradition and supporters of the established "imperialist" government—a conflict that resulted in a determination by parents to seize control of their children's education. Following the period of discord, the people of Akwesasne came together around the vision of the school, which began to focus on the reclamation of cultural identity and the Mohawk language. White illustrates how AFS educates through a holistic philosophy in which "all aspects of a person are central to understanding human behavior, and the interrelationship of all living things is recognized" (79). Values such as respect, cooperation, and kinship are taught through ceremony, song, dance, and nature. Students learn from teachers, parents, elders, and one another, and the Mohawk language (Kanienke:ha) is central to all learning that takes place.

The second half of the book focuses on the revitalization of Kanienke:ha. White discusses the precarious state of Indigenous languages due to colonization, assimilation practices, and cultural genocide. She acknowledges the community-level struggle between Native language and English before asserting the necessity for language immersion in schools as a mechanism to produce fluent speakers and create opportunity for language practice. Referencing interviews with students and parents, White describes the school as an agent of language renewal that "provides hope that Mohawk language and culture will survive for the next seven generations" (121). Language, then, becomes White's catalyst for "becoming Mohawk." She builds her argument for the development of identity by emphasizing the link between language and culture, which she says "shapes how we see and understand the world around us" (135–36). Finally, White discusses becoming "fully Mohawk," a condition she relates to being fully human, a process that White believes is exemplified at Akwesasne Freedom School, where, through language and culturally relevant study, Mohawk students "fulfill their human potential and find personal meaning" (169).

Free to Be Mohawk is an enjoyable read that is accessible to both Native and non-Native readers. White provides a poignant example of the power of language in the creation of identity, at both the individual and the community level. She also demonstrates the power of a culturally relevant curriculum for Indigenous youth. At times, White seems noncommittal about whether becoming "fully Mohawk" requires a return to the traditional Longhouse way of life, but she clearly acknowledges the complex nature of religion, culture, language, and tradition that the people of Akwesasne still face. White's first book is an important contribution to the field of Indigenous education, not only because it chronicles a fully self-sufficient and self-determined school, but also because it demonstrates the important role of education in decolonization efforts. With this work, White provides a valuable resource for Indigenous peoples who seek to use schools as agents of cultural renewal and true self-determination as well as scholars interested in Mohawk sovereignty.

ANTHONY SNETHEN is a Ph.D. student in education policy studies at the University of Kansas.

KATHRYN WALKIEWICZ

Indigenous Passages to Cuba, 1515–1900
by Jason M. Yaremko
University Press of Florida, 2016

JASON YAREMKO'S *Indigenous Passages to Cuba, 1515–1900* demonstrates how Indigenous peoples navigated networks of "mobility, migration, and diaspora" throughout the Caribbean and across North America in response to colonialism (164). More specifically, he invites us to rethink how colonialism forced some Amerindians far from their ancestral homelands but nonetheless situated them as important actors in Cuban history. Yaremko provides an account of heterogeneous Cuban Indigeneity, which he describes as the "multicultural or multinational indigenous presence in colonial Cuba," and argues that Cuba (and often Havana more specifically) serves as a central site for understanding histories of Indigenous diaspora, diplomacy, labor, and forced migration of Amerindians (142). *Indigenous Passages* argues that rather than being a place where Indigenous people were completely eradicated, as the colonial narrative fantasy often goes, Cuba economically *depended* on the labor of a diasporic Indigenous population well into the twentieth century.

Partly due to missionary efforts, and partly due to Indigenous migration and diplomacy, Havana became an important node on Indigenous circuits of migration, exile, and mobility in the seventeenth and eighteenth centuries. In this way we might understand Havana as a "Native hub," to use Renya Ramirez's term, or a place that operated as a locus for Indigenous engagement with Spanish empire. As Yaremko is careful to insist, however, these thoroughfares and circuits of movement and exchange were dictated as much by Indigenous peoples as they were by the Spanish. Chapter 1 details Spain's fairly fruitless attempts to missionize Indigenous peoples in Florida. Instead of developing a mission network across the territory that would secure colonial control, Yaremko describes how, time and again, leaders from the Calusa and other Indigenous communities in La Florida would request Spanish missionary assistance with ulterior motives that had less to do with desires for conversion and more to do with securing a colonial ear for diplomatic negotiating. Despite Spanish attempts to regulate the spiritual, political, and economic lives of Indigenous populations in Florida and Cuba, Indigenous peoples used understandings of Spanish colonial governance to negotiate to their own ends whenever possible.

In the second through fifth chapters of *Indigenous Passages*, Yaremko explains that Havana served as a significant destination for Indigenous peoples, in some cases by choice and in others by forced relocation. Havana was a nexus of African slavery and Spain's imperial defense, shipping, and trade in the Americas and, as such, a strategic site for speaking back to empire. Indigenous people of the continental Southeast, particularly Muscogee/ Creek communities, maintained relationships with Spain even after Spain conceded control of the region. Indigenous leaders and delegates continued to travel back and forth to Havana, protecting mutually beneficial economic and political relationships and, for Creek delegates, acquiring needed resources and weapons to stave off increasing French, British, and (later) U.S. interference. However, as Yaremko explains in chapters 3 and 4, not all "Amerindians" traveled to Havana as diplomats. Apaches, Mecos, Yucatec Maya, and others were forcibly sent to Cuba in an attempt to weaken the threat posed to continental New Spain by repeated Indigenous uprisings, attacks, and warfare in opposition to colonialism, and later by the Mexican republic. Amerindian deportees provided additional labor to an economy in constant need of a larger workforce and became desirable domestic workers, seen as less costly and racially less threatening than black slaves. Yaremko spends the final chapters of his book detailing Yucatec Maya life in Cuba and the ways Maya advocated for themselves and their communities, especially as an often-exploited labor workforce.

While this book opens up questions about Indigenous diasporas, mestizaje nationalisms, transits, and continental intimacies, it does not actively engage these topics or the work of Indigenous studies (or Caribbean diasporic studies) scholars who are invested in similar lines of inquiry. This seems a missed opportunity, as dialogue with works by Jodi Byrd, James Cox, Shari Huhndorf, María Josefina Saldaña-Portillo, and Jace Weaver (to name only a few) would serve as compelling interlocutors to reinforce Yaremko's key claims about the heterogeneity of Indigenous place making. Additionally, Yaremko spends very little time in the text accounting the histories of Arawak Taíno communities and offers only a brief reference to recent and continued efforts by Taíno activists and scholars to insist on their continued presence in Cuba. Nonetheless, *Indigenous Passages* provides a rich historical account of Cuban Indigenous diasporas that powerfully depicts the scope and complexity of transnational Indigenous social relations in the Americas.

KATHRYN WALKIEWICZ is an assistant professor in the Literature Department at the University of California San Diego.

ERIC CHEYFITZ

Uncivil Rites: Palestine and the Limits of Academic Freedom
Haymarket Press, 2015
by Steven Salaita

AT THE CENTER OF *Uncivil Rites* is Steven Salaita's precise and thorough commentary on his firing in August of 2014 from the University of Illinois at Urbana-Champaign after his hiring by the university's American Indian Studies Program, a hire approved in late September of 2013 by the interim dean, Brian H. Ross. Professor Salaita accepted the position in early October, resigned his tenured position at Virginia Tech, and in the summer of 2014 was preparing to move his family to Champaign when on August 1 he was peremptorily fired before he ever got to assume his position as associate professor with tenure. The letter of termination, signed by Chancellor Phyllis M. Wise and Vice President for Academic Affairs Christophe Pierre, gives no reason for the termination but simply refers to a *pro forma* sentence in the dean's letter offering the position to Salaita: "This recommendation for appointment is subject to approval by the Board of Trustees of the University of Illinois." The citing of this sentence was followed by the blow: "We write to inform you that your appointment will not be recommended for submission to the Board of Trustees." This letter and the dean's letter along with a letter from then acting director of the American Indian Program, Dr. Jodi Byrd, outlining the terms of the hire are reprinted in the appendix of Salaita's book. They are important reading for those who want to understand the institutional violence in this case.

Salaita's firing, then, was a violation of expected university hiring practices, where the faculty and the dean are typically entrusted with such decisions. Thus, the peremptory firing constitutes a subversion of faculty governance, departmental/program autonomy, and, as it turned out, Professor Salaita's academic freedom. For the firing, as subsequent events made abundantly clear, was based on Salaita's principled stand in support of Palestinian rights, particularly his support of Palestinian civil society's nonviolent Boycott, Divestment, and Sanctions movement (BDS) aimed at legally resisting Israeli colonialism. A particular irony in this regard is that the dean's letter offering the position to Salaita contained the following boilerplate: "At the University of Illinois, like most universities in this country, we subscribe to the principles of academic freedom and tenure laid down by the American Association of University Professors (AAUP)."

Forced to come up with some reason for his termination, then, the administration cited Professor Salaita's "uncivil" Twitter feed in support of

Palestinian rights as a reason to deem him unfit to be a teacher and colleague at Illinois, even though his record on both counts at Virginia Tech was impeccable and even though extramural speech is protected under the canons of academic freedom developed by the AAUP, which invoked those canons in unequivocally condemning Chancellor Wise's decision, driven by the Board of Trustees backed by certain university donors. But of course the administration's emphasis in criticizing Salaita's Twitter feed was on his "incivility," not on his criticism of Israeli state policy because the Illinois administration had to try to maintain the increasingly transparent illusion that universities are supporters of academic freedom and diversity in all matters.

Salaita does a splendid job of deconstructing this particular fiction, while analyzing the limits of academic freedom so evident in his case and others. In this respect chapter 1, "Tweet Tweet," opens with the question "Does Twitter lend itself to civility?" Salaita's answer is emphatically "no." Nor, he explains, is Twitter intended to be a platform for civility. Nor, for that matter, is it anybody's business under both the First Amendment and the canons of academic freedom to judge a discourse's "civility," whatever that word may mean. To explore this meaning, which he does with incisive analysis in the course of the book, Salaita focuses on the colonial origins of the word "civility," its precise use in the discourse of "savagery" to distinguish "them" from "us." As Salaita remarks: "Civility exists in the lexicon of conquest. It is the language of Cotton Mather's diatribes. It is the discourse of educated racism. It is the sanctimony of the authoritarian. It is the pretext of the oppressor" (105). And in understanding the global dimensions of his particular case, Salaita comments on the reach of colonialism in Israeli-occupied Palestine and U.S.-occupied Indian country into the academy (and he rightly links these two colonialisms):

> That I was hired to teach in American Indian Studies is crucial because my termination isn't simply a personal problem, but a representation of the marginal standing of American Indian and Indigenous Studies (and the humanities and social sciences more broadly). That university administrators deployed the language of civility in the wake of its decision illuminates a model of governance deeply rooted in colonial ethos. (105)

Uncivil Rites is an important book for furthering our understanding of the colonial reach of the corporate university.

ERIC CHEYFITZ is Earnest I. White Professor of American Studies and Humane Letters at Cornell University.

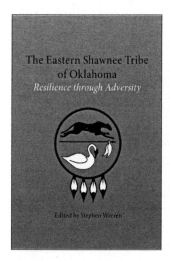

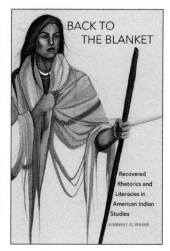

NEW FROM MINNESOTA

As We Have Always Done
Indigenous Freedom through Radical Resistance
Leanne Betasamosake Simpson

"This is an astonishing work of Indigenous intellectualism and activism—by far the most provocative, defiant, visionary, and generous of Leanne Betasamosake Simpson's impressive corpus to date." —**Daniel Heath Justice** (Cherokee Nation), University of British Columbia

$24.95 hardcover | 320 pages | Indigenous Americas Series

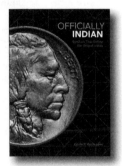

The River Is in Us
Fighting Toxics in a Mohawk Community
Elizabeth Hoover

"Elizabeth Hoover's rich ethnography will leave an enduring mark on the field of Indigenous environmental studies."
—Clint Carroll (Cherokee Nation), author of Roots of Our Renewal

$28.00 paper | $112.00 cloth | 392 pages
27 b&w photos

Officially Indian
Symbols that Define the United States
Cécile Ganteaume
Foreword by Colin G. Calloway
Afterword by Paul Chaat Smith

A wide-ranging exploration of the symbolic importance of American Indians in the visual language of U.S. democracy

$28.00 hardcover | 192 pages | 50 color photos

The Sioux Chef's Indigenous Kitchen
Sean Sherman
With Beth Dooley

"A cookbook meant to be studied, one where the recipes are not its most important feature, but rather a part of an overall call to reclaim the history and culture of indigenous peoples."
—Foreword Reviews, starred review

$34.95 hardcover | 240 pages | 6 b&w photos
115 color photos

Onigamiising
Seasons of an Ojibwe Year
Linda LeGarde Grover

"A finely nuanced reflection on the spiritual and the mundane, the everyday and the extraordinary, the seasons of the year and the seasons of a life." —Indian Country Today

$14.95 paper | 216 pages

University of Minnesota Press | www.upress.umn.edu | 800-621-2736

wicazō ṡa review

A Journal of Native American Studies

James Riding In, Editor

"*Wicazo Sa Review* is one of the core titles in Native American studies." —*Magazines for Libraries*

"With depictions of indigenous races continuing to promote stereotypes, a serious dialogue like the one presented here is a necessity. Recommended for all libraries." —*Ulrich's Periodicals Directory*

The essential source for new thought in Native American studies.

During the past two decades, Native American Studies has emerged as a central arena in which Native American populations in the United States define the cultural, religious, legal, and historical parameters of scholarship and creativity essential for survival in the modern world. Founded in 1985, *Wicazo Sa Review* is a journal in support of this particular type of scholarship, providing inquiries into the Indian past and its relationship to the vital present. Its aim is to become an interdisciplinary instrument to assist indigenous peoples of the Americas in taking possession of their own intellectual and creative pursuits.

Wicazo Sa Review is published twice a year in spring and fall and is available online

Manuscripts for submission and books for review should be addressed to:

James Riding In, Wicazo Sa Review
American Indian Studies
Arizona State University
PO Box 874603
Tempe, AZ 85287-4603

Subscription information is available at:
http://www.upress.umn.edu/journal-division/Journals/wicazo-sa-review

Journal of American Indian Education

Editors:
Bryan McKinley Jones Brayboy,
Teresa L. McCarty,
and K. Tsianina Lomawaima

Original scholarship on indigenous education issues

Founded in 1961, the *Journal of American Indian Education* (*JAIE*) features original scholarship on education issues of American Indians, Alaska Natives, Native Hawaiians, and Indigenous peoples worldwide, including First Nations, Māori, Aboriginal/ Torres Strait Islander peoples, and Indigenous peoples of Latin America, Africa, and others.

JAIE is published three times per year.
Submission guidelines and subscription information available at:
http://www.upress.umn.edu/journal-division/Journals/journal-of-american-indian-education